A VAMPIRE'S LOVE A MURDER MYSTERY E A MURDER MYSTERY

DOUG HENSLEY

A VAMPIRE'S LOVE A MURDER MYSTERY E A MURDER MYSTERY

Ingram spark

CONTENTS

A Vampire's Love

A Murder Mystery

By

Doug Hensley

Table Of Contents

Chapter 15: The Final Clue
Chapter 16: The Chase
Chapter 18: The Tur
Chapter 19: The Confrontation
Chapter 20: Redemption
Chapter 1: A Stranger in Town

The townsfolk eyed the mansion on the edge of town, long shrouded in mystery, as it suddenly gained life. A chilling wind accompanied the newcomer, whose presence sent shivers down the spines of those unlucky enough to cross his path.

The mansion, with its creaking gates and twisted, overgrown gardens, seemed to moan in protest as the stranger took resi-dence. Rumors spread like wildfire—some said he was a wealthy recluse, while others whispered darker tales of the supernatural.

The stranger, a tall figure draped in shadows, went by the name of Victor Blackwood. He was pale as the moon, his eyes like shards of obsidian that seemed to pierce through the darkest corners of one's soul. Victor's arrival coincided with a peculiar change in the air—a heaviness that crept through the town, unsettling its once-peaceful atmosphere.

As Victor settled into the mansion, he acquired control of the local funeral home, a place already shrouded in the echoes of sorrow. The townspeople, accustomed to grieving in hushed tones, now found themselves uneasy in the face of this enigmatic figure orchestrating their final farewells.

The funeral home, once a sanctuary for solace, transformed into an eerie realm under Victor's influence. Candles flickered with an unnatural glow, casting unsettling shadows on the walls. Whispers of strange rituals and macabre ceremonies spread through the town, heightening the fear that clung to Ravenshade like a lingering fog.

Victor Blackwood, the puppeteer of grief, moved with an un-settling grace, his eyes gleaming with an otherworldly hunger.

The townspeople began to notice a strange occurrence—a chilling sensation that crawled down their spines whenever Victor passed by. They exchanged wary glances, unsure if it was merely superstition or something far more sinister.

As the stranger's presence settled in Ravenshade, the once close-knit community unraveled. Unexplained noises echoed from the mansion, and the nights seemed to grow longer as fear seeped into the hearts of the townsfolk. Whispers of strange happenings reached every corner of Ravenshade, fueling the town's collective anxiety.

Little did they know, this was just the beginning of a tale that would weave together love, mystery, and the haunting specter of an ancient darkness. The stranger's arrival had set in motion a chain of events that would challenge the very fabric of reality in Ravenshade, leaving its inhabitants to confront their deepest fears and darkest desires.

Chapter 2: The Funeral Director

The town of Ravenshade awoke to an atmosphere fraught with tension, an unspoken unease that hung thick in the air like an impending storm. Victor Blackwood, now known as the mysterious funeral director, wielded his influence over the local funeral home with an eerie mastery that sent shivers down the spines of grieving families.

The once-familiar funeral home, a place of solace and remembrance, transformed into a macabre theater under Victor's command. The air within its walls seemed charged with an otherworldly energy, as if the grieving process itself had become a stage for something darker.

Victor, draped in a shadowy elegance, moved among the mourners with an uncanny grace. His piercing eyes, like twin abysses, seemed to absorb the sorrow of those who sought comfort within the dimly lit halls. Candles flickered in strange patterns, casting elongated shadows that danced eerily on the walls.

Grieving families, already burdened with the weight of loss, found themselves at the mercy of the funeral director's unsettling presence. Whispers of strange rituals conducted behind closed doors circulated through the town like wildfire, each tale more chilling than the last. Mourners spoke of cryptic symbols etched onto caskets and mournful chants that echoed through the night.

The townspeople, once united in shared grief, now became isolated in their fear. Families hesitated to approach the funeral home, choosing instead to mourn their loved ones in private. The communal rituals that had once brought solace now seemed tainted by an unseen malevolence.

As Victor continued to preside over the funeral home, an air of dread settled over Ravenshade. Strange occurrences accompanied his every step—the distant wailing of unseen specters, shadows that seemed to move of their own accord, and an unrelenting cold that permeated the very walls of the building.

Rumors spread of Victor's ability to commune with the deceased, whispering secrets only the departed could know. Families, desperate for closure, sought his services, unaware of the darkness that clung to the funeral director like a cloak. The line between the living and the dead blurred, and the town became a breeding ground for fear and suspicion.

The once-thriving community found itself fractured, torn apart by the ominous presence that had taken root in its heart. The funeral home, once a pillar of solace, now stood as a foreboding symbol of the encroaching darkness. And as the townspeople grappled with their grief, they couldn't shake the unsettling feeling that they were mere pawns in a sinister game orchestrated by the enigmatic funeral director, Victor Blackwood.

Chapter 3: Love at First Sight

In the midst of Ravenshade's growing fear, a glimmer of hope emerged in the form of a beautiful woman named Isabella

Hartfield. Isabella, with her flowing auburn hair and eyes that sparkled like sunlight on water, seemed like a beacon of warmth in the encroaching darkness.

Isabella frequented the town square, where the marketplace bustled with life despite the pall that hung over Ravenshade. She caught the attention of Victor Blackwood, the mysterious funeral director whose gaze had always been cold and distant. However, as he observed Isabella, something stirred within him—a feeling long forgotten, an ember of humanity flickering amidst the shadows.

Isabella, unaware of the town's growing apprehension, carried herself with an air of grace that intrigued Victor. As their eyes met across the crowded square, a connection sparked, setting into motion a series of events that would forever alter the fate of Ravenshade.

Victor, compelled by an unfamiliar yearning, found himself drawn to Isabella like a moth to a flame. He watched her from the shadows, a silent observer of her daily life. Isabella, in turn, couldn't shake the feeling of being watched, an unsettling sensation that sent shivers down her spine.

Their paths eventually crossed during a chance encounter at the local bookstore. Isabella, browsing the shelves of worn paperbacks, felt a sudden chill in the air. She turned to find Victor standing there, his dark eyes locked onto hers. The air crackled with an unspoken energy—an inexplicable connection that transcended the ordinary.

As Isabella and Victor exchanged pleasantries, an undeniable chemistry simmered beneath the surface. It was a dance of words and glances, each moment charged with an unspoken tension. Isabella, though initially wary of the enigmatic funeral director, felt a strange pull toward him that she couldn't ignore.

Their interactions became a secret affair, hidden from the prying eyes of the town. Isabella found herself entangled in a web of emotions she couldn't comprehend—a fascination with the mysterious man who seemed to straddle the line between the living and the dead.

As their connection deepened, Isabella's presence became a source of solace for Victor, a flicker of light in his shadowy existence. But the townspeople, already on edge, began to take notice of the budding relationship. Whispers spread like wildfire, casting a darker shadow over the couple.

The air in Ravenshade crackled with a palpable tension—a brewing storm of fear, love, and uncertainty. Isabella and Victor, entangled in a love that defied the boundaries of the known, would soon find themselves at the center of a tempest that threatened to tear the fabric of their reality apart. Little did they know that the threads of their fate were intricately woven with the ominous mysteries lurking in the shadows of Ravenshade.

Chapter 4: Forbidden Desires

In the heart of Ravenshade, where the shadows clung to every corner and the air crackled with an unspoken tension, the forbidden romance between Isabella and Victor unfolded. As their connection deepened, the town's apprehension grew, like a storm gathering strength on the horizon.

Isabella, with her radiant smile and gentle spirit, found herself captivated by Victor's enigmatic charm. His eyes, once cold and distant, now softened in her presence. They stole moments together in the moonlit gardens, where whispers of their love danced with the rustling leaves.

But love in Ravenshade was a perilous endeavor, and the couple couldn't escape the watchful eyes of the townspeople. Rumors of their entanglement spread through the community like wildfire, fueled by the fear that clung to the air. Gossip became a weapon, and the couple found themselves at the center of a storm they had not anticipated.

As the town's anxiety mounted, Isabella and Victor faced a growing chorus of disapproval. Friends turned strangers, and neighbors exchanged wary glances whenever the couple passed by. The air, once thick with the scent of blooming flowers, now carried the acrid undertone of fear.

Isabella, torn between her growing love for Victor and the disapproval of the town, found herself caught in a web of conflicting emotions. Victor, haunted by the specter of his own dark secrets, grappled with the weight of bringing danger to the woman he had come to cherish.

One fateful night, as a tempest brewed overhead, Isabella and Victor sought refuge in the mansion's dimly lit halls. The thunder roared, drowning out the distant murmurs of the townspeople. It was a night where passion and fear collided—a night that would shape the destiny of Ravenshade.

In the shadows of the mansion, with the storm raging outside, Isabella confronted Victor about the whispers that had reached her ears. The accusations of his involvement in the mysterious deaths that haunted the town. Victor, his gaze haunted by a thousand regrets, revealed a truth that sent shivers down Isabella's spine.

He was not just a man; he was something else—something that existed in the liminal space between life and death. A creature cursed with an insatiable thirst for human blood. Isabella, torn between terror and love, grappled with the revelation, her heart pounding like a drum in the dark.

As the storm raged on, Isabella made a choice that defied reason. Instead of recoiling in horror, she embraced Victor, vowing to stand by his side against the encroaching darkness. Their love became a beacon, a fragile flame flickering in the face of a malevolent force that sought to tear them apart.

Little did they know, their decision to confront the truth together would set in motion a series of events that would test the limits of their love and the strength of their resolve. The storm outside mirrored the tempest within Ravenshade—a town on the brink of unraveling, where forbidden desires collided with the harsh reality of a world haunted by the unknown.

Chapter 5: A Series of Murders

In the aftermath of the stormy night that had forever changed Isabella and Victor, Ravenshade plunged into a deeper darkness. The air became charged with an oppressive heaviness, and the town's once-familiar streets felt like a labyrinth of uncertainty.

As whispers of the forbidden love between Isabella and Victor lingered, a more ominous shadow fell upon Ravenshade—a series of mysterious deaths that sent shockwaves through the community. The victims, one by one, met their demise in ways that left the townspeople trembling with fear and suspicion.

The first death, that of old Mr. Jenkins, a kind soul who had lived in Ravenshade for decades, occurred under circumstances that defied explanation. His lifeless body, drained of color, was discovered in his home. The air carried a scent of decay, and the townspeople exchanged fearful glances, realizing that something unnatural had occurred.

The second victim, a young florist named Emily, met a similar fate. Her body was found in the moonlit cemetery, surrounded by wilting flowers and an eerie silence that seemed to echo with the weight of the unknown. Fear tightened its grip on Ravenshade, and rumors of a malevolent force grew louder.

The third death struck even closer to home. Mary, the baker known for her warm heart and delicious pastries, was found lifeless in her kitchen. The once-pleasant aroma of freshly baked bread now mingled with the stench of death. Panic spread through the town like wildfire, as the realization set in that a serial killer—or something far more sinister—stalked the streets of Ravenshade.

Detective Martin Harris, a seasoned investigator with a gruff exterior, took charge of the case. The murders, with their inexplicable nature, fueled his determination to bring the killer to justice. As he delved into the investigation, Detective Harris couldn't ignore the undercurrent of fear that permeated the once-peaceful town.

Victor, with his unsettling connection to the funeral home and the recent revelation of his vampiric nature, became a person of interest in the detective's eyes. The townspeople, gripped by paranoia, pointed accusatory fingers at the mysterious funeral director, further intensifying the atmosphere of dread.

Isabella, torn between her love for Victor and the mounting fear gripping the town, found herself entangled in a web of conflicting emotions. She witnessed the accusatory glares and heard the hushed whispers that painted Victor as the perpetrator. Yet, her heart refused to accept the possibility that the man she loved could be capable of such horrors.

As the body count rose, the town's collective anxiety reached a fever pitch. Every creaking floorboard and rustling leaf became a harbinger of doom, and the once-cozy streets now felt like a haunting maze. Ravenshade, once a haven of community, had become a place of fear, suspicion, and unspeakable horrors.

In the face of the escalating nightmare, Isabella and Victor found themselves standing at the crossroads of love and terror. As Detective Harris closed in on the truth, the couple realized that time was running out. They had to confront the malevolent force that haunted Ravenshade, unravel the mysteries that bound them, and somehow find a way to stop the relentless tide of death that threatened to drown the town in darkness.

Chapter 6: The Detective's Hunch

Ravenshade, gripped by the grim specter of a series of mysterious deaths, became a town shrouded in fear. The once-familiar streets now echoed with the hushed whispers of its frightened inhabitants. Detective Martin Harris, a weathered figure with a determination etched into the lines of his face, found himself thrust into a case that defied rational explanation.

The first murder, that of Mr. Jenkins, had left a haunting imprint on Detective Harris. As he examined the scene, a gnawing unease settled in the pit of his stomach. The lack of discernible motive and the eerie circumstances surrounding the deaths were like pieces of a puzzle that refused to fit together.

The detective, known for his pragmatic approach, couldn't shake the feeling that there was more to these murders than met the eye. Each crime scene bore a sinister signature—a peculiar arrangement of shadows, an inexplicable coldness, and an air thick with the stench of death. As he delved deeper into the investigation, Detective Harris sensed that he was treading on the edge of something far beyond the scope of his understanding.

The townspeople, already on edge from the string of deaths, cast wary glances at each other. Whispers of a malevolent force lurking in the shadows spread through Ravenshade like wildfire. The once-cohesive community now teetered on the brink of paranoia, and the detective became acutely aware of the fear that pulsed through the town's veins.

Victor Blackwood, the mysterious funeral director, had become a person of interest in Detective Harris's investigation. The townspeople, driven by a collective hysteria, pointed accusatory fingers at the enigmatic figure who had taken residence on the outskirts of town. The detective, skeptical but compelled by the mounting evidence, began to scrutinize Victor's every move.

As Detective Harris questioned Victor and probed the funeral home's secrets, a chilling revelation emerged—the connection between the deaths and the eerie occurrences at the mansion. The detective's hunch intensified, and a grim suspicion crept into his mind. Could Victor Blackwood be more than just a bystander in this macabre puzzle?

Isabella, caught between her love for Victor and the rising tide of suspicion, found herself torn. The detective's inquiries cast a shadow over the fragile sanctuary she had built with Victor. The town, gripped by fear, watched the unfolding drama with bated breath.

Detective Harris, driven by an unrelenting determination to uncover the truth, became haunted by dreams that blurred the line between reality and nightmare. Visions of shadowy figures and blood-stained corridors tormented his nights, leaving him on edge during waking hours. The once-sturdy detective felt the tendrils of an unseen force wrapping around him, urging him to unveil the malevolence that lurked beneath Ravenshade's surface.

The investigation took a darker turn when Emily, the young florist, became the latest victim. The townspeople, now consumed by panic, demanded swift justice. The detective, fueled by a sense of urgency, intensified his scrutiny of Victor Blackwood. Every piece of evidence, every sidelong glance, and every cryptic detail pointed toward the funeral director as the epicenter of the town's descent into madness.

As Detective Harris closed in on Victor, Isabella and her beloved found themselves caught in the eye of the storm. The town, torn between fear and a desperate need for answers, stood on the precipice of a revelation that would either shatter the illusions of normalcy or plunge Ravenshade into an abyss of eternal darkness. The detective's hunch, though fraught with uncertainty, had become a relentless force propelling him toward a confrontation that would test the limits of his convictions and unveil the true horrors that lurked in the shadows of Ravenshade.

Chapter 7: Love Blossoms

In the looming shadow of Detective Harris's intensifying investigation, Ravenshade became a town gripped not only by fear but also by the blossoming tendrils of forbidden love. Isabella and

Victor, entangled in a romance that defied reason, found solace in each other's arms amidst the encroaching darkness.

As the detective continued to scrutinize Victor's every move, the couple sought refuge in the sanctuary of the mansion. The walls, though adorned with ornate tapestries, seemed to whisper secrets of the ancient darkness that lurked within. Isabella and Victor, in the quiet moments stolen from the town's judgmental gaze, found a fragile oasis where love could flourish despite the gathering storm.

The mansion's gardens, once vibrant with life, became a clandestine meeting place for the couple. Flowers bloomed in hues of blood-red and midnight black, mirroring the intensity of their emotions. The moon, a silent witness to their clandestine meetings, bathed the lovers in its soft glow as they exchanged vows of devotion and faced the uncertainties that loomed over Ravenshade.

Yet, even in the refuge of their love, the town's suspicion cast a long, chilling shadow. Isabella, torn between her loyalty to Victor and the fear of losing him, faced the challenge of shielding their love from the prying eyes of the townspeople. The once-familiar faces now bore expressions of judgment, and the couple's stolen moments became increasingly fraught with the looming threat of exposure.

Detective Harris, driven by an unrelenting determination to solve the baffling murders, grew ever closer to unraveling the secrets that the mansion held. Every visit to Victor's funeral home yielded more questions than answers, and the detective couldn't shake the feeling that he was on the verge of a revelation that would shake Ravenshade to its core.

Isabella, caught in the crossfire of love and fear, became the emotional fulcrum upon which the town's destiny teetered. Her heart, entwined with Victor's, bore the weight of secrets that threatened to unravel everything they held dear. The mansion, once a symbol of Victor's mysterious allure, now became a crucible where love and darkness collided.

The townspeople, fueled by a collective paranoia that mirrored Detective Harris's suspicions, began to rally against the perceived threat that Victor posed. An air of tension gripped the once-cohesive community, and the streets buzzed with speculative murmurs. The fear, palpable in the air, manifested as accusatory glances and hushed conversations that painted Victor Blackwood as the embodiment of the town's deepest nightmares.

As the couple faced the mounting pressure from all sides, their love deepened into a bond that transcended the mortal coil. Isabella, despite the chaos that surrounded them, stood steadfast beside Victor. The funeral director, haunted by the weight of his own existence, found solace in the warmth of Isabella's unwavering love.

But love in Ravenshade, tainted by the fear of the unknown, became a fragile thread that threatened to snap under the strain. The mansion, once a refuge, now echoed with the footsteps of impending doom. The town, on the brink of collective hysteria, stood at the crossroads of love and horror, where the choices made by Isabella and Victor would determine not only their fate but the fate of Ravenshade itself. As Detective Harris closed in on the truth, the lovers clung to each other, hoping that their love could withstand the tempest that raged within and beyond the haunted walls of the mansion.

Chapter 8: The Vampire's Dilemma

As the moon cast an eerie glow over Ravenshade, the town teetered on the precipice of dread. Detective Harris's investigation, fueled by a relentless determination to unearth the truth, cast a long shadow over Victor Blackwood and the forbidden love he shared with Isabella. In the mansion on the outskirts, where the air hummed with ancient secrets, the vampire faced an internal dilemma that threatened to unravel the fragile tapestry of his existence.

Victor, haunted by the specter of his own nature, grappled with the burden of his insatiable thirst for human blood. The once-cold eyes that had softened in Isabella's presence now reflected the torment within. The mansion, with its twisting corridors and dimly lit chambers, became a prison of conflicting desires—an eternal struggle between the man who longed for love and the creature that craved the darkness.

Isabella, sensing the turmoil that consumed Victor, became a steadfast pillar of support. Their love, though tested by the town's suspicions and the detective's relentless pursuit, held a fragility that transcended the mortal realm. But the vampire's dilemma cast a looming shadow over their moments of stolen tenderness.

As Detective Harris unearthed more clues that pointed towards Victor's involvement in the mysterious deaths, the town's paranoia escalated. Whispers of dark rituals and malevolent forces echoed through the streets, painting the funeral director as the harbinger of doom. The once-thriving community now stood at the brink of collective hysteria, with fear coiling around every corner like a venomous serpent.

Victor, burdened by the weight of his existence, confided in Isabella about the curse that bound him—a curse that demanded the lifeblood of the living. The revelation sent shockwaves through her, and the couple found themselves entangled in a love that transcended the boundaries of mortality. Isabella, torn between the man she loved and the monstrous truth he harbored, faced a choice that would shape the destiny of Ravenshade.

The mansion's walls, adorned with portraits of faces long lost to time, seemed to echo with the agonized whispers of the undead. Victor, desperate to find a way to quell his bloodlust and protect the woman he loved, delved into forbidden tomes and ancient scrolls. The library, a repository of arcane knowledge, held the key to a solution that could either free Victor from his vampiric chains or condemn him to an eternity of darkness.

Detective Harris, unaware of the supernatural forces at play, closed in on the funeral home with a determination that mirrored the inexorable march of fate. The evidence, though circumstantial, pointed towards Victor as the elusive thread connecting the deaths that plagued Ravenshade. The town, perched on the precipice of hysteria, clamored for justice as the vampire's dilemma deepened.

Isabella, caught between the detective's relentless pursuit and Victor's struggle for redemption, became the emotional fulcrum upon which the fate of Ravenshade swayed. The couple, united by a love that defied reason, faced a race against time to unravel the mysteries that bound them and find a way to quench the insatiable thirst that threatened to consume Victor's soul.

As the mansion's chambers echoed with the whispered incantations of forgotten lore, and the detective closed in on the truth, the vampire's dilemma intensified. The town, unaware of the supernatural forces that governed their destinies, stood on the brink of revelation. In the heart of Ravenshade, where love and horror danced a macabre waltz, the choices made by Isabella, Victor, and Detective Harris would determine whether the town would succumb to the shadows or find a glimmer of salvation in the midst of the encroaching darkness.

Chapter 9: The Investigation Heats Up

Ravenshade, enveloped in a shroud of fear and suspicion, felt the town's heartbeat quicken as Detective Martin Harris intensified his pursuit of the truth. The series of mysterious deaths, the forbidden love between Isabella and Victor, and the looming presence of an ancient darkness cast a pall over the community. As Detective Harris delved deeper into the investigation, the air became thick with tension, and the town's collective anxiety reached a fevered pitch.

The detective, driven by an unyielding determination to solve the baffling murders, sifted through the clues like a bloodhound on the scent. Every visit to Victor's funeral home unearthed more questions than answers, and the whispers that painted the enigmatic funeral director as the harbinger of doom grew louder. The once-cohesive community now stood divided, with suspicions tearing through the fabric of trust that had bound Ravenshade together.

Isabella, torn between her love for Victor and the detective's relentless pursuit, found herself caught in a whirlwind of conflicting emotions. The mansion, once a sanctuary, now echoed with the haunting whispers of secrets long buried. The town's scrutiny intensified

Chapter 10 Unraveling Secrets

The darkness clung to Ravenshade like a malevolsent force as Detective Martin Harris pressed on with his investigation, fueled by an unyielding determination to untangle the web of mysteries that gripped the town. The air crackled with tension, and the once-close-knit community now stood on the precipice of revelation.

Detective Harris, armed with the fragments of evidence he had gathered, delved into the funeral home's murky secrets. The flickering candles, the ominous undertones, and the whispers of forbidden rituals painted Victor Blackwood as a figure of suspicion. As the detective sifted through the shadows, the walls seemed to close in around him, whispering secrets that sent shivers down his spine.

Isabella, caught in the crossfire of the investigation, felt the weight of the town's gaze bearing down on her. The once-hidden love between her and Victor now stood exposed, a fragile flame flickering against the encroaching darkness. The mansion's halls, once a sanctuary for their stolen moments, echoed with the haunting footsteps of Detective Harris, each stride bringing them closer to the heart of the mysteries that bound Ravenshade.

Victor, tormented by his dual nature, grappled with the knowledge that his very existence was a threat to the town and the woman he loved. The library, a repository of forbidden knowledge, beckoned him to seek a solution that would sever the ties between his vampiric curse and the string of deaths that haunted Ravenshade.

As Detective Harris followed the trail of clues, the town's paranoia heightened. Whispers of curses, supernatural entities, and the malevolent influence of the funeral director spread like wildfire. The once-thriving streets now bore the weight of fear, and the townspeople exchanged furtive glances as shadows played tricks on their senses.

Isabella, in her desperate attempt to shield Victor from the detective's scrutiny, sought answers within the mansion's ancient tomes. The pages, filled with cryptic symbols and arcane incantations, hinted at a dark history that transcended time. With each revelation, the couple's love became a beacon in the gathering storm, a flicker of hope against the encroaching night.

Detective Harris, unbeknownst to him, stood at the threshold of the mansion's secrets. The detective's hunch, driven by a relentless pursuit of justice, led him to confront Victor in the dimly lit chambers where the air seemed to vibrate with suppressed power. Isabella, torn between her loyalty to Victor and the looming threat of exposure, stood on the precipice of a revelation that could shatter the fragile peace that remained in Ravenshade.

The mansion, a silent witness to the unfolding drama, held the key to the town's salvation or damnation. The detective's footsteps echoed through the corridors, each one carrying the weight of impending confrontation. As the secrets of Ravenshade's dark tapestry unraveled, the town stood on the edge of a precipice, where the choices made in the coming moments would determine the destiny of its inhabitants and the fate of the love that dared to bloom in the face of an ancient, malevolent force.

Chapter 11: Confrontation in the Shadows

Ravenshade, a town gripped by fear and secrets, found itself at a pivotal moment as Detective Martin Harris closed in on the enigma that was Victor Blackwood. The detective's footsteps echoed through the dimly lit corridors of the mansion, and the air seemed to hum with the weight of impending revelation. Isabella, torn between her love for Victor and the looming confrontation, felt the town's destiny hang in the balance.

Detective Harris, fueled by the fragments of evidence and the relentless pursuit of justice, approached Victor in the heart of the mansion. The funeral director, his eyes reflecting the torment within, awaited the inevitable confrontation. The room felt charged with an otherworldly energy as the detective, unaware of the supernatural forces at play, prepared to unveil the mysteries that had cast a shadow over Ravenshade.

Isabella, standing at the intersection of love and dread, watched as the two figures faced each other. The detective's accusing gaze met Victor's haunted eyes, and in that moment, the mansion's walls seemed to pulse with an ancient heartbeat. The air crackled with tension as the detective began to question Victor about the deaths that haunted the town.

Victor, caught between the weight of his vampiric nature and the desire to protect Isabella, felt the walls closing in around him. The detective's questions were a relentless assault, each inquiry tearing at the fragile facade that concealed the dark truths within. Isabella, unable to bear the strain, clutched the edges of her reality, her heart pounding with a rhythm that echoed through the mansion.

As the confrontation unfolded, the shadows themselves seemed to dance with malevolence. Whispers of forgotten curses and the thirst for blood intertwined with the detective's accusations, creating a symphony of dread that reverberated through the once-hallowed halls. The mansion, a repository of ancient secrets, bore witness to a clash between mortal justice and the supernatural forces that lurked within.

In the midst of the confrontation, Isabella, desperate to shield Victor, revealed the depths of their forbidden love. The confession hung in the air, a revelation that added another layer to the town's collective horror. The detective, now entangled in a web of love and darkness, grappled with the realization that the enigmatic funeral director was not merely a suspect but a creature torn between worlds.

The town, oblivious to the supernatural drama unfolding, trembled on the brink of chaos. The whispers of a malevolent force echoed through the streets, and the air seemed to thicken with an unspoken dread. The choices made in the mansion's dimly lit chambers would ripple through Ravenshade, shaping its fate and the destinies of those entwined in the macabre tapestry of love and horror.

As the confrontation reached its climax, the mansion's secrets threatened to spill into the town's consciousness like a tidal wave of revelation. Isabella, Victor, and Detective Harris stood at the epicenter of a storm that would either consume Ravenshade in darkness or expose the truth that had long languished in the shadows. The drama that unfolded within those walls would leave an indelible mark on the town, forever altering the course of its history.

Chapter 12: The Pact of Shadows

The revelation of Victor's vampiric nature and Isabella's forbidden love had plunged Ravenshade into a maelstrom of horror and uncertainty. Detective Martin Harris, still grappling with the supernatural truth, stood at the crossroads of mortal justice and the ancient darkness that clung to the town. As the trio confronted the secrets within the mansion's walls, the air pulsed with an ominous energy, foretelling a climax that would resonate through Ravenshade's very soul.

The detective, eyes wide with disbelief, demanded answers from Victor. The funeral director, his features etched with a mixture of guilt and defiance, hesitated before weaving a tale of curses, immortal thirst, and centuries-old shadows. Isabella, her heart pounding in rhythm with the town's collective fear, pleaded for understanding as the revelations unfolded like a nightmarish tapestry.

Within the dimly lit chambers, the mansion seemed to rebel against the weight of its own secrets. Shadows danced with an eerie sentience, contorting into shapes that whispered forgotten horrors. The detective's interrogation became a dance with the unknown, each revelation more horrifying than the last. The very fabric of reality seemed to fray as the trio navigated the treacherous terrain between the living and the undead.

As Victor recounted his cursed existence, the detective's skepticism clashed with the supernatural truths that defied logic. Isabella, caught in the crossfire, felt the tension escalate like a storm on the horizon. The mansion, a silent witness to centuries of secrets, bore witness to the fragility of mortal understanding in the face of immortal mysteries.

In the shadows, an ancient force stirred—a malevolence that transcended time and clung to Victor like a symbiotic curse. The town, unaware of the supernatural tempest that raged within the mansion, trembled on the brink of a revelation that would either shatter the illusions of normalcy or plunge it into an abyss of eternal darkness.

As the detective continued his relentless pursuit of truth, Isabella and Victor faced a dilemma that mirrored the town's uncertainty. Could the vampire's insatiable thirst for blood be quenched, and was redemption possible for a creature that had straddled the line between life and death for centuries? The answers, buried in the cryptic tomes of the mansion's library, eluded them like elusive specters.

The air within Ravenshade became charged with an unspoken pact—a covenant between shadows and the living. The mansion's secrets, once bound by the veils of time, threatened to rupture the fragile balance between the mundane and the supernatural. Isabella, Victor, and Detective Harris stood at the nexus of this cosmic struggle, each choice echoing through the town like a tolling bell.

As the confrontation neared its climax, the mansion's halls seemed to close in, trapping the trio in a labyrinth of revelations and uncertainty. The choices made within those walls would determine not only the fate of Victor and Isabella but also the destiny of Ravenshade itself. In the heart of the macabre drama, where love and horror danced an intricate waltz, the town stood on the brink of a revelation that would either herald salvation or plunge it into an abyss of eternal night.

Chapter 13: A Pact with Darkness

The air within Ravenshade remained thick with tension as the revelation of Victor's vampiric nature unfolded in the dimly lit chambers of the mansion. Detective Martin Harris, still grappling with the unearthly truth, found himself caught between the pursuit of justice and the incomprehensible horrors that seemed to weave themselves into the fabric of the town. Isabella and Victor, entwined in a love that defied the boundaries of mortality, stood at the epicenter of a cosmic struggle that threatened to consume them all.

As the detective pressed Victor for more details, the funeral director spoke of an ancient curse that bound him to the shadows—a curse that demanded the lifeblood of the living. Isabella, her heart heavy with the weight of forbidden love and supernatural revelations, pleaded for understanding. The mansion, a repository of arcane knowledge, seemed to echo with the collective gasp of a town on the brink of unraveling.

The detective's skepticism clashed with the supernatural truths that defied reason. The very foundation of reality trembled as Victor's tale unfolded like a sinister lullaby. In the flickering candlelight, the shadows contorted into grotesque shapes, mirroring the torment within the immortal being who stood at the center of the unfolding drama.

As the trio navigated the labyrinth of revelations, an ancient force stirred in the shadows—a malevolence that had haunted Ravenshade for centuries. The mansion, a silent witness to a pact with darkness, seemed to breathe with a sentience that transcended time. Isabella, Victor, and the detective stood at the threshold of a cosmic reckoning, where the choices made would resonate through the town's very soul.

Isabella, torn between her love for Victor and the fear that gripped the town, sought answers within the dusty tomes of the mansion's library. The pages whispered of forbidden rituals, of curses that transcended generations, and of a way to sever the ties that bound Victor to the insatiable thirst for blood. The library, once a haven of knowledge, now felt like a portal to the abyss.

Detective Harris, his mind a battleground of rationality and supernatural revelation, grappled with the notion that the creature standing before him was more than a suspect—it was a force that defied the laws of nature. The detective's resolve wavered as the walls seemed to close in, each revelation pulling him deeper into the abyss of the unknown.

As the tension reached its zenith, a pact with darkness emerged—an unspoken agreement between the living and the undead. The mansion's ancient secrets threatened to spill into the town like a cascade of shadows, challenging the fragile equilibrium that had masked the supernatural truths for centuries.

In the heart of Ravenshade, where mortal and immortal forces collided, Isabella, Victor, and Detective Harris faced a choice that would shape the destiny of the town. The air crackled with an otherworldly energy as they grappled with the implications of the revelations. The mansion's chambers, once a sanctuary, now felt like a crucible where the town's fate would be forged in the fires of an ancient, malevolent force.

As the trio stood at the crossroads of love and horror, the town held its breath, unaware of the cosmic drama that played out within the haunted walls of the mansion. The choices made within those dimly lit chambers would echo through Ravenshade's history, determining whether the town would succumb to the encroaching darkness or find a glimmer of salvation in the midst of the supernatural storm.

Chapter 14: Veil of Shadows Unveiled

The revelation of Victor's vampiric nature had plunged Ravenshade into a maelstrom of fear and uncertainty. The town, once shrouded in a deceptive sense of normalcy, now stood at the precipice of an abyss, where the supernatural and mortal collided in a cosmic dance of dread. As Isabella, Victor, and Detective Martin Harris grappled with the unfolding horrors within the mansion, the air vibrated with an otherworldly tension.

Victor, haunted by the weight of his immortal existence, stood as a living paradox—a creature of the night who longed for the warmth of love. Isabella, torn between loyalty to her beloved and the looming threat that Victor posed to the town, felt the burden of an impossible choice. Detective Harris, caught in the crossfire of supernatural revelation and mortal duty, stood as a lone bastion against the encroaching darkness.

Within the dimly lit chambers, the trio confronted the ancient force that stirred in the shadows. Victor, his eyes reflecting centuries of torment, spoke of a pact with darkness—a curse that bound him to an insatiable thirst for human blood. The detective, though still grappling with disbelief, felt the weight of supernatural truths closing in like a vice.

As Isabella sought answers within the dusty tomes of the mansion's library, the pages revealed a path to redemption. Whispers of ancient rituals and forgotten incantations hinted at a way to sever the vampiric curse that gripped Victor's soul. The library, a repository of secrets, became a battleground where the forces of salvation and damnation clashed.

The mansion itself seemed alive with the echoes of centuries gone by. The walls pulsed with an otherworldly energy, and the very air seemed to breathe with sentience. Shadows danced with malevolence, contorting into nightmarish shapes that mirrored the internal struggles of those within. The choices made within those walls would reverberate through the town's history.

Detective Harris, torn between the pursuit of justice and the supernatural revelations that defied reason, faced a test of resolve. The evidence of Victor's vampiric nature seemed irrefutable, yet the detective grappled with the knowledge that the town stood on the brink of a truth that transcended mortal understanding.

Isabella, armed with the newfound knowledge from the ancient tomes, confronted Victor with the possibility of breaking the curse. The mansion's chambers became a crucible where love and redemption clashed with the ancient malevolence that lurked in the shadows. The choices made by the trio would determine whether Ravenshade would be condemned to eternal night or find a glimmer of hope amidst the encroaching darkness.

As the confrontation reached its climax, the mansion's secrets threatened to spill into the town's consciousness. The very foundation of reality trembled, and Ravenshade stood at the crossroads of salvation and damnation. Isabella, Victor, and Detective Harris faced a cosmic reckoning, their fates intertwined with the town's destiny in ways they could not yet comprehend.

The air crackled with an intensity that mirrored the town's collective fear. In the heart of Ravenshade, where love and horror had become inseparable, the trio prepared to make a final stand against the ancient force that sought to claim their souls. The choices made within those haunted walls would echo through eternity, sealing the town's fate in a veil of shadows that veiled the truth in mystery and dread.

Chapter 15: The Descent into Darkness

Ravenshade, now ensnared in a web of unearthly revelations, stood on the precipice of a descent into the unknown. As Isabella, Victor, and Detective Martin Harris grappled with the implications of the vampiric curse and the potential for redemption, the town's pulse quickened with a shared fear that hung in the air like a looming storm. The mansion, a crucible of love, horror, and ancient malevolence, became the stage for a final act that would determine Ravenshade's destiny.

Isabella, armed with the esoteric knowledge gleaned from the mansion's library, shared her findings with Victor. The ritual to break the curse loomed before them, a glimmer of hope in the encroaching darkness. Detective Harris, torn between skepticism and the undeniable supernatural truths, stood witness to a cosmic struggle that transcended the bounds of mortal understanding.

The trio, bound by fate and the choices that lay ahead, entered the mansion's ritual chamber. Candles flickered ominously, casting dancing shadows that seemed to whisper of the ancient forces at play. The air hummed with an eerie energy as the town's destiny unfolded within those dimly lit walls.

Victor, the weight of centuries etched on his features, faced the ritual with a mixture of desperation and determination. Isabella, torn between love and the fear of what Victor might become, stood steadfast at his side. Detective Harris, though still skeptical, sensed the gravity of the moment—a moment that could tip the scales between salvation and damnation.

As the ritual began, the mansion seemed to come alive with an unseen force. Shadows writhed and contorted, casting grotesque silhouettes on the chamber walls. The town, unaware of the supernatural drama unfolding, felt an unspoken unease that permeated the very fabric of Ravenshade.

The ritual's incantations echoed through the chamber, and the air became charged with an otherworldly tension. Isabella's voice, trembling yet resolute, mingled with the supernatural whispers that seemed to seep from the very stones of the mansion. The detective, caught in the crossfire of ancient forces, could feel the town's fate hanging in the balance.

As the ritual reached its crescendo, a palpable darkness descended upon the chamber. Victor, his features contorted in pain, bore the weight of the ritual's transformative power. Isabella, her heart pounding with a mixture of hope and fear, clung to the belief that love could conquer even the darkest curses.

Suddenly, an otherworldly scream pierced the air—a sound that seemed to echo through the ages. The mansion's walls shook, and the very ground beneath Ravenshade quivered. The town, now aware of an unseen turmoil, stood on the edge of collective hysteria.

Isabella, her eyes fixed on Victor, witnessed a transformation that defied the laws of nature. The ritual's outcome remained uncertain, and the shadows that clung to the chamber seemed to pulse with an ancient malevolence. Detective Harris, his skepticism waning in the face of the supernatural spectacle, felt the weight of the town's fear pressing down upon him.

In the heart of Ravenshade, where mortal and immortal forces clashed in a final, dramatic confrontation, the choices made within the ritual chamber would determine the town's fate. The air crackled with an intensity that mirrored the collective pulse of the townspeople, unaware of the battle that raged within the haunted walls of the mansion. As the ritual's echoes reverberated through Ravenshade, the town held its breath, suspended in a moment that would either usher in a new dawn or plunge them into an eternal night.

Chapter 16: Shadows Unleashed

Ravenshade, teetering on the brink of an otherworldly revelation, held its breath as the ritual within the mansion's chamber reached its crescendo. Isabella, Victor, and Detective Martin Harris stood at the epicenter of a cosmic struggle, where love and horror clashed in the dimly lit sanctuary. The air pulsed with an intensity that mirrored the collective fear of a town thrust into the heart of supernatural upheaval.

The ritual's incantations reverberated through the chamber, casting an eerie glow on the faces of those entwined in its mystical dance. Isabella, her voice intermingling with the arcane whispers, clung to the belief that the ritual could sever Victor's vampiric curse. The detective, his skepticism eroding in the face of the unfolding spectacle, sensed the town's fate hanging in the balance.

As the ritual's power surged, the mansion seemed to come alive with an unseen force. Shadows, once confined to the corners, writhed and contorted like malevolent specters. The very foundation of the town trembled, and an unspoken unease settled over Ravenshade like a shroud of impending doom.

Victor, caught in the throes of transformation, emitted an otherworldly scream that seemed to pierce the veil between the mortal and the supernatural. Isabella, her heart wrenching at the sight of his torment, clutched onto hope as the ritual's arcane energies wove through the fabric of his being. The detective, torn between duty and the supernatural forces at play, could feel the town's collective anxiety pressing upon him like a weight.

Suddenly, the chamber erupted in a burst of blinding light—a radiance that seemed to defy the oppressive darkness that had haunted Ravenshade. The town, now aware of an unseen turmoil, stood on the brink of collective hysteria as the mansion's ancient secrets threatened to spill into the streets.

As the light subsided, the chamber fell into an eerie stillness. Isabella's eyes, wide with anticipation, sought Victor amidst the lingering shadows. The detective, bracing for the unknown, felt the weight of the town's destiny pressing upon him like an insurmountable burden.

Victor emerged from the ritual's aftermath, his features transformed but free from the vampiric pallor that had defined him for centuries. Isabella, a mixture of relief and awe in her eyes, rushed to his side. The mansion, still bathed in an otherworldly aura, seemed to exhale a sigh of ancient secrets unveiled.

The town, oblivious to the supernatural drama within the mansion, stood on the cusp of revelation. Isabella, Victor, and Detective Harris emerged from the chamber, their faces etched with the indelible marks of a cosmic confrontation. The air, now thick with uncertainty, carried whispers of change that wafted through Ravenshade's streets like a haunting melody.

Isabella, her hand entwined with Victor's, faced the town that had become a crucible of love and horror. The detective, still grappling with the unearthly truths that defied reason, braced for the aftermath of the ritual. Ravenshade, a town forever altered by the events within the mansion, held its breath as the trio stepped into the unknown, where the shadows of the past had been unleashed, and the future hung in the delicate balance between light and darkness.

Chapter 17: Echoes of Redemption

The aftermath of the ritual lingered over Ravenshade like a ghostly apparition, casting an unsettling stillness over the town. Isabella, Victor, and Detective Martin Harris emerged from the mansion's chamber, their faces a tapestry of emotions. The air crackled with an unspoken tension, and the town stood on the edge of a revelation that pulsed through the very heart of Ravenshade.

Isabella, her hand tightly clasped with Victor's, faced the wary gazes of the townspeople. The couple, now transformed by the ritual's mysterious energies, became a living enigma in the eyes of those who had only glimpsed the shadows of their secrets. Detective Harris, still grappling with the supernatural truths that defied his rational mind, observed the unfolding drama with a sense of trepidation.

Ravenshade, oblivious to the cosmic struggle that had played out within the mansion, felt the lingering echoes of change. Whispers of the ritual's aftermath spread through the streets, like an invisible current carrying tales of redemption and supernatural forces transcending mortal understanding. The town, once cocooned in the familiarity of everyday life, now stood at the crossroads of normalcy and the unknown.

Isabella, sensing the town's collective gaze, stood firm. The love between her and Victor, now freed from the vampiric curse, became a beacon in the encroaching darkness. The mansion, once a harbinger of fear, now held the promise of redemption—an enigma that the townspeople could neither comprehend nor ignore.

Detective Harris, torn between duty and the supernatural truths he had witnessed, felt the weight of the town's uncertainty pressing upon him. The evidence of the ritual's transformative power stood before him, challenging the very foundations of his understanding of the world. The detective, haunted by the shadows of the unknown, braced for the inevitable questions that would cascade through Ravenshade like a tidal wave.

As the trio ventured into the town's heart, they encountered curious glances and hushed conversations. The air seemed to thicken with a palpable tension as the townspeople grappled with the implications of the supernatural events that had unfolded within the mansion. Ravenshade, a town steeped in ancient secrets, now faced a reckoning that would shape its destiny.

Isabella, guided by a newfound strength, addressed the townspeople. She spoke of redemption, of breaking the shackles of ancient curses, and of the transformative power of love. The mansion, once a symbol of fear, became a testament to the resilience of the human spirit against the encroaching shadows.

The detective, though still skeptical, sensed the sincerity in Isabella's words. The town, caught between fear and the allure of redemption, stood at the precipice of a collective decision. As Isabella and Victor's love became a rallying point, the streets of Ravenshade echoed with a chorus of uncertainty and anticipation.

The mansion, bathed in the glow of newfound hope, stood as a silent witness to the town's transformation. The shadows that had haunted its corridors for centuries seemed to retreat, leaving behind the echoes of an ancient struggle that had reached its climax. Ravenshade, a town forever changed, faced a future that bore the indelible marks of a cosmic drama that had played out within its very heart.

As the trio navigated the streets, they became unwitting symbols of a supernatural redemption that defied the expectations of mortal understanding. The town, now poised between skepticism and the allure of a new beginning, grappled with the aftermath of the ritual that had unraveled the tapestry of its secrets. In the heart of Ravenshade, where love and horror had danced a macabre waltz, the choices made by Isabella, Victor, and Detective Harris would ripple through the town's history, shaping its future in the lingering echoes of redemption.

Chapter 18: Unveiling the Abyss

The aftermath of the ritual lingered over Ravenshade like a ghostly mist, leaving the town caught between the allure of redemption and the ever-present shadows of uncertainty. Isabella,

Victor, and Detective Martin Harris became unwitting symbols of a supernatural transformation that defied the logic of everyday life. The air crackled with an unspoken tension, and the town stood on the precipice of revelation, unsure of what lay beyond the veils of the unknown.

Isabella, her hand still entwined with Victor's, faced the wary gazes of the townspeople. The couple, marked by the aftermath of the ritual, became an enigma that both fascinated and frightened the community. Detective Harris, still grappling with the supernatural truths that had unraveled within the mansion, observed the unfolding drama with a sense of trepidation.

Ravenshade, now privy to the echoes of the ritual's aftermath, buzzed with speculation and fear. Whispers of the transformative power of the ritual spread like wildfire through the streets, conjuring images of redemption and the supernatural forces that had, until now, lurked in the shadows. The town, once shielded by the mundane, now stood exposed to the abyss that yawned beneath the surface.

Isabella, sensing the town's collective gaze, felt the weight of expectation and fear. The love she shared with Victor, now freed from the vampiric curse, became both a beacon and a harbinger of the unknown. The mansion, once a dwelling of fear, now stood as a gateway to the mysteries that Ravenshade had long sought to bury.

Detective Harris, torn between his duty as an officer of the law and the supernatural reality that defied his understanding, grappled with the uncertainty that pervaded the town. The detective, once a bastion of rationality, now stood at the precipice of an abyss that threatened to swallow the very fabric of his beliefs.

As the trio moved through the town, they encountered a mixture of curiosity and trepidation. The air seemed thick with an invisible tension as the townspeople wrestled with the implications of the supernatural events that had unfolded within the mansion.

Ravenshade, a town shackled by ancient secrets, now faced the daunting task of confronting the abyss that had opened within its very heart.

Isabella, guided by a newfound strength, addressed the townspeople once more. She spoke of redemption, of the transformative power of the ritual, and of the love that had defied the darkness. The mansion, now both a symbol of fear and hope, echoed with Isabella's words, and the town listened with a collective sense of awe and trepidation.

The detective, though still skeptical, found himself caught in the undertow of Isabella's sincerity. The town, standing at the crossroads of skepticism and the allure of a new beginning, grappled with the aftermath of the ritual that had unraveled the tapestry of its secrets. Ravenshade, a town forever changed, faced a future that held the indelible marks of a cosmic drama that had played out within its very core.

As the trio moved through the streets, they became reluctant heralds of a supernatural redemption that defied the expectations of the mortal realm. The town, now standing at the brink of an uncertain future, wrestled with the aftermath of the ritual that had laid bare the shadows of its own existence. In the heart of Ravenshade, where love and horror had danced their intricate waltz, the choices made by Isabella, Victor, and Detective Harris would echo through the town's history, leaving behind a legacy that would forever haunt the collective consciousness of the community.

Chapter 19: The Fraying Veil

Ravenshade, once shrouded in mystery, now stood exposed to the aftermath of the transformative ritual. Isabella, Victor, and Detective Martin Harris became both witnesses and participants in a drama that unfolded within the streets and minds of the town. The air vibrated with a sense of uncertainty, as if the fabric hanging precariously on the edge of the unknown.

Isabella, holding Victor's hand tightly, felt the weight of the town's collective gaze. The ritual had changed them, and the town, uncertain of the nature of this transformation, teetered on the edge of fear and fascination. Detective Harris, still grappling with the supernatural truths, sensed the tension that clung to the air like a suffocating mist.

Rumors and whispers about the trio's encounter with the supernatural spread like wildfire through Ravenshade. The streets, once familiar and comforting, now buzzed with an unsettling energy. The townspeople, caught between skepticism and the lingering shadows of the ritual, awaited the next chapter in a story that had unraveled the very fabric of their existence.

Isabella, recognizing the town's need for understanding, decided to address the community once more. Standing in the town square, she spoke of the ritual's purpose, of breaking the shackles of ancient curses, and of love as the guiding force that had brought them to this moment. The mansion, looming in the background, seemed to watch over the unfolding drama, its walls echoing with the secrets that had been laid bare.

Detective Harris, torn between duty and the supernatural forces at play, observed the crowd. The detective, once the embodiment of law and order, now grappled with the unknown, unsure of how to restore a semblance of normalcy to a town caught in the throes of the extraordinary.

As Isabella's words resonated through the square, a sudden chill swept through Ravenshade. The atmosphere thickened, and an oppressive darkness seemed to claw its way into the hearts of the townspeople. Whispers of an ancient malevolence, awakened by the ritual, slithered through the air like a serpent ready to strike.

Unseen by the crowd, shadows gathered at the periphery, forming grotesque shapes that danced in the corners of perception. The town's newfound hope began to waver, and a sense of foreboding settled over Ravenshade like a shroud. The supernatural forces, once thought to be quelled, now threatened to unravel the fragile peace that had briefly settled upon the town.

Isabella, sensing the shift in the atmosphere, felt a knot tighten in her stomach. Victor, by her side, gripped her hand with a newfound intensity. Detective Harris, his instincts tingling with an eerie premonition, scanned the surroundings, searching for the source of the encroaching darkness.

Suddenly, a piercing scream shattered the uneasy calm. A figure emerged from the shadows, distorted and contorted, a manifestation of the malevolence that had been unleashed. The townspeople recoiled in horror as the once-familiar face twisted into a grotesque mask of supernatural malevolence.

Panic spread through the square like wildfire. The fraying veil between the known and the unknown tore open, and the townspeople, once united by curiosity and fear, now scattered in terror. The supernatural forces, emboldened by the disturbance, manifested in eerie shapes that slithered through the streets, leaving a trail of horror in their wake.

Isabella, Victor, and Detective Harris found themselves at the center of a maelstrom. The mansion, once a symbol of redemption, now seemed like a gateway to a realm of nightmares. The trio, burdened by the consequences of the ritual, stood amidst the chaos, grappling with the realization that the forces they had awakened were far more malevolent than they could have ever imagined.

As the shadows tightened their grip on Ravenshade, the town, once again, found itself thrust into a relentless battle between the supernatural and the mundane. The choices made in the aftermath of the ritual would determine whether the fragile threads holding the town together would unravel completely or if a new, more terrifying tapestry would be woven in the darkness that had been unleashed.

Chapter 20: Embrace of Shadows

Ravenshade, plunged into chaos by the unforeseen malevolence, trembled on the brink of a nightmarish abyss. Isabella, Victor, and Detective Martin Harris stood as unwitting architects of the supernatural forces that now clawed at the very fabric of their reality. The air, once filled with whispers of redemption, now echoed with the wails of terror and the palpable darkness that seeped into every corner.

As the malevolent figure emerged from the shadows, the town square became a theater of horror. The once-tranquil streets transformed into a maze of fear, with panicked townspeople fleeing from the twisted manifestation of supernatural malevolence. The trio, their faces etched with horror, braced themselves for the onslaught of forces they had inadvertently unleashed.

The mansion, a looming silhouette against the night sky, seemed to watch the chaos unfold with an eerie stillness. The walls, once witnesses to centuries of secrets, now bore witness to the repercussions of tampering with forces beyond mortal comprehension. Isabella, Victor, and Detective Harris found themselves ensnared in a struggle that transcended the boundaries of the known.

The malevolent figure, a grotesque embodiment of ancient shadows, slithered through the square, leaving a trail of dread in its wake. Its contorted features spoke of a darkness that defied the laws of nature, and the very air seemed to ripple with an unsettling energy. Ravenshade, now a battleground between the forces of light and darkness, quivered under the weight of an impending nightmare.

Isabella, her heart pounding with a mixture of guilt and determination, locked eyes with Victor. The love that had once been a beacon of hope now faced a trial by fire. Detective Harris, the stalwart figure caught between the mundane and the supernatural, drew his weapon with a newfound urgency, ready to confront the malevolence that threatened to consume the town.

The townspeople, caught in the throes of panic, sought refuge wherever they could find it. The streets, once bustling with the everyday rhythm of life, now reverberated with the frenzied footsteps of those desperate to escape the encroaching darkness. Windows shuttered, doors slammed shut, and the once-cordial neighbors became strangers bound by a shared terror.

The trio, guided by instinct, led the charge against the malevolent force. The mansion's shadowy facade loomed ahead, a symbolic threshold between the known and the unknown. Isabella, her voice trembling yet resolute, urged the townspeople to rally together in the face of the supernatural onslaught.

As the malevolent figure closed in, the mansion's ancient secrets seemed to pulse with a malevolent glee. The walls, etched with the echoes of centuries, bore witness to the unraveling of a delicate balance. Isabella, Victor, and Detective Harris faced a choice—stand united against the shadows or succumb to the abyss that threatened to swallow Ravenshade whole.

The malevolent figure, sensing the resistance, unleashed a barrage of supernatural horrors. Shadows twisted and contorted, taking on monstrous forms that danced with an unnatural malevolence. The town's fate hung in the balance, teetering between salvation and damnation.

In the heart of Ravenshade, where the air crackled with an intensity that mirrored the collective fear, the trio confronted the malevolent force. The mansion, once a symbol of redemption, now stood as a battleground where the choices made would determine whether the town could emerge from the embrace of shadows or be forever consumed by the darkness that had been unleashed.

The malevolent force surged forward, its shadowy tendrils reaching out like insidious fingers, seeking to ensnare the hearts and minds of those it touched. The town square became a chaotic battleground, with the trio at the forefront, desperately trying to push back the encroaching darkness.

Isabella, her voice cutting through the dissonance, urged the townspeople to stand together against the malevolence. A fragile alliance formed amidst the chaos, with fear-stricken faces looking to the trio for guidance. The mansion, its ancient walls now a silent witness to the unfolding nightmare, seemed to exude a spectral energy that heightened the stakes of the cosmic struggle.

Detective Harris, his resolve hardened by the urgency of the situation, coordinated efforts to fortify the town square. Makeshift barricades were erected, and the echoes of gunfire reverberated through the night as the townspeople, armed with whatever they could find, prepared to face the malevolent force.

Victor, once burdened by his vampiric curse, now stood as a stalwart defender alongside Isabella. The love that had once been a source of redemption now became a beacon of resistance against the encroaching shadows. As the malevolent force bore down on them, the trio faced the realization that the consequences of their actions had ignited a supernatural war within the heart of Ravenshade.

The malevolent figure, now an amorphous mass of darkness, oozed through the barricades, evading conventional understanding. It whispered ancient incantations, unsettling the resolve of those who stood against it. The air, thick with a malevolent energy, seemed to pulse with the heartbeat of an otherworldly power.

The mansion, once a refuge of arcane knowledge, now revealed its true nature. Its corridors, twisted by the malevolence, became a labyrinth of shifting shadows and unforeseen horrors. Isabella, guided by an instinct that seemed to transcend mortal understanding, led the charge into the mansion, hoping to find a way to quell the supernatural onslaught.

As they delved into the mansion's depths, they encountered spectral manifestations and illusions that twisted the fabric of reality. Each step seemed to take them further into a nightmarish realm, where time and space became fluid, and the boundaries between the living and the supernatural blurred.

Detective Harris, his skepticism now replaced by a grim determination, faced the malevolent force head-on. The town's fate hung in the balance, and with every passing moment, the struggle intensified. The air, once thick with the stench of fear, now resonated with the battle cries of those who dared to challenge the abyss.

Isabella, Victor, and Detective Harris, their journey through the mansion fraught with terror and uncertainty, stumbled upon an ancient chamber at the heart of the building. A ghastly altar, adorned with arcane symbols, pulsed with an ominous energy. It became apparent that the mansion itself harbored the malevolent force, and severing its connection to the supernatural realm became the key to saving Ravenshade.

As the trio prepared to confront the malevolence at its source, the town square outside echoed with the desperate struggle of the townspeople. The battle against the shadows had become a test of resilience, where the choices made within the mansion would determine whether Ravenshade could emerge from the embrace of darkness or succumb to an eternal night.

In the ancient chamber at the heart of the mansion, Isabella, Victor, and Detective Harris confronted the malevolence that had taken residence

within its walls. The air felt heavy with the weight of unseen forces, and the trio braced themselves for a confrontation that would shape the town's destiny.

The altar, a macabre centerpiece of the supernatural energies that had tainted the mansion, pulsed with an otherworldly glow. Symbols etched into the stone seemed to writhe, and the very air shimmered with an unnatural energy. Isabella, drawing upon the knowledge gained from the ancient tomes, recognized that severing the connection between the mansion and the malevolent force was their only hope.

As they approached the altar, the malevolence manifested itself in a ghastly form—a shadowy apparition that seemed to draw from the darkest recesses of the human psyche. It whispered ancient curses, amplifying the fears and doubts of those who stood before it. Isabella, fortified by the love she shared with Victor, resisted the insidious whispers, determined to break the hold of the supernatural malevolence.

Victor, once tormented by his vampiric nature, found newfound strength in the face of the malevolence. The love he felt for Isabella became a shield against the shadows, and he stood alongside her, ready to confront the darkness that threatened to consume Ravenshade.

Detective Harris, a beacon of mortal resilience in the supernatural storm, gripped his weapon tightly. The detective, now fully aware of the extraordinary forces at play, faced the malevolence with a steadfast resolve. The town's fate rested on their shoulders, and the ancient chamber became the battlefield where mortal and supernatural clashed.

Isabella, her voice resonating with ancient incantations, began a ritual to sever the mansion's connection to the malevolent force. The air crackled with energy as the symbols on the altar reacted to the arcane power coursing through the room. Shadows recoiled, and the malevolent apparition writhed in agony, its form flickering like a dying flame.

The battle outside the mansion raged on. In the town square, the townspeople, armed with a newfound determination, faced the shadowy manifestations that sought to engulf Ravenshade. The air echoed with the sounds of struggle, the clash of improvised weapons, and the desperate cries of those fighting for their homes and loved ones.

As Isabella's ritual intensified, the mansion itself seemed to rebel against the malevolence. The walls groaned, and ethereal whispers filled the air. Detective Harris, sensing the pivotal moment, urged the townspeople to stand firm, reinforcing the barricades against the malevolent forces that threatened to spill out of the mansion.

Suddenly, a blinding light erupted from the altar, illuminating the chamber with an intensity that banished the shadows. Isabella, Victor, and Detective Harris felt the surge of power as the ritual reached its climax. The malevolent force, writhing in its death throes, let out a deafening scream that reverberated through the mansion.

In the town square, the townspeople witnessed the sudden stillness of the shadows. The malevolent apparitions dissipated, leaving behind an eerie calm. Ravenshade, once consumed by chaos, seemed to exhale as the supernatural threat lifted.

As the light from the altar subsided, Isabella, Victor, and Detective Harris emerged from the ancient chamber. The mansion, once a nexus of darkness, now stood silent, its secrets laid bare. The trio, weary yet triumphant, stepped into the town square, where the townspeople greeted them with a mixture of awe and gratitude.

Ravenshade, though scarred by the supernatural ordeal, stood on the threshold of a new beginning. Isabella, Victor, and Detective Harris, their journey through love, horror, and redemption now etched into the town's history, faced a community that had witnessed the extraordinary. The choices made within the mansion had sealed the town's fate, and as Ravenshade began to rebuild, the echoes of the supernatural struggle would linger as a cautionary tale—a reminder of the delicate balance between light and darkness.

A Vampire's Love
A Murder Mystery
By
Doug Hensley
Table Of Contents

Chapter 1: A Stranger in Town

The townsfolk eyed the mansion on the edge of town, long shrouded in mystery, as it suddenly gained life. A chilling wind accompanied the newcomer, whose presence sent shivers down the spines of those unlucky enough to cross his path.

The mansion, with its creaking gates and twisted, overgrown gardens, seemed to moan in protest as the stranger took residence. Rumors spread like wildfire—some said he was a wealthy recluse, while others whispered darker tales of the supernatural.

The stranger, a tall figure draped in shadows, went by the name of Victor Blackwood. He was pale as the moon, his eyes like shards of obsidian that seemed to pierce through the darkest corners of one's soul. Victor's arrival coincided with a peculiar change in the air—a heaviness that crept through the town, unsettling its once-peaceful atmosphere.

As Victor settled into the mansion, he acquired control of the local funeral home, a place already shrouded in the echoes of sorrow. The townspeople, accustomed to grieving in hushed tones, now found themselves uneasy in the face of this enigmatic figure orchestrating their final farewells.

The funeral home, once a sanctuary for solace, transformed into an eerie realm under Victor's influence. Candles flickered with an unnatural glow, casting unsettling shadows on the walls. Whispers of strange rituals and macabre ceremonies spread through the town, heightening the fear that clung to Ravenshade like a lingering fog.

Victor Blackwood, the puppeteer of grief, moved with an unsettling grace, his eyes gleaming with an otherworldly hunger.

The townspeople began to notice a strange occurrence—a chilling sensation that crawled down their spines whenever Victor passed by. They exchanged wary glances, unsure if it was merely superstition or something far more sinister.

As the stranger's presence settled in Ravenshade, the once close-knit community unraveled. Unexplained noises echoed from the mansion, and the nights seemed to grow longer as fear seeped into the hearts of the townsfolk. Whispers of strange happenings reached every corner of Ravenshade, fueling the town's collective anxiety.

Little did they know, this was just the beginning of a tale that would weave together love, mystery, and the haunting specter of an ancient darkness. The stranger's arrival had set in motion a chain of events that would challenge the very fabric of reality in Ravenshade, leaving its inhabitants to confront their deepest fears and darkest desires.

Chapter 2: The Funeral Director

The town of Ravenshade awoke to an atmosphere fraught with tension, an unspoken unease that hung thick in the air like an impending storm. Victor Blackwood, now known as the mysterious funeral director, wielded his influence over the local funeral home with an eerie mastery that sent shivers down the spines of grieving families.

The once-familiar funeral home, a place of solace and remembrance, transformed into a macabre theater under Victor's command. The air within its walls seemed charged with an otherworldly energy, as if the grieving process itself had become a stage for something darker.

Victor, draped in a shadowy elegance, moved among the mourners with an uncanny grace. His piercing eyes, like twin abysses, seemed to absorb the sorrow of those who sought comfort within the dimly lit halls. Candles flickered in strange patterns, casting elongated shadows that danced eerily on the walls.

Grieving families, already burdened with the weight of loss, found themselves at the mercy of the funeral director's unsettling presence. Whispers of strange rituals conducted behind closed doors circulated through the town like wildfire, each tale more chilling than the last. Mourners spoke of cryptic symbols etched onto caskets and mournful chants that echoed through the night.

The townspeople, once united in shared grief, now became isolated in their fear. Families hesitated to approach the funeral home, choosing instead to mourn their loved ones in private. The communal rituals that had once brought solace now seemed tainted by an unseen malevolence.

As Victor continued to preside over the funeral home, an air of dread settled over Ravenshade. Strange occurrences accompanied his every step—the distant wailing of unseen specters, shadows that seemed to move of their own accord, and an unrelenting cold that permeated the very walls of the building.

Rumors spread of Victor's ability to commune with the deceased, whispering secrets only the departed could know. Families, desperate for closure, sought his services, unaware of the darkness that clung to the funeral director like a cloak. The line between the living and the dead blurred, and the town became a breeding ground for fear and suspicion.

The once-thriving community found itself fractured, torn apart by the ominous presence that had taken root in its heart. The funeral home, once a pillar of solace, now stood as a foreboding symbol of the encroaching darkness. And as the townspeople grappled with their grief, they couldn't shake the unsettling feeling that they were mere pawns in a sinister game orchestrated by the enigmatic funeral director, Victor Blackwood.

Chapter 3: Love at First Sight

In the midst of Ravenshade's growing fear, a glimmer of hope emerged in the form of a beautiful woman named Isabella

Hartfield. Isabella, with her flowing auburn hair and eyes that sparkled like sunlight on water, seemed like a beacon of warmth in the encroaching darkness.

Isabella frequented the town square, where the marketplace bustled with life despite the pall that hung over Ravenshade. She caught the attention of Victor Blackwood, the mysterious funeral director whose gaze had always been cold and distant. However, as he observed Isabella, something stirred within him—a feeling long forgotten, an ember of humanity flickering amidst the shadows.

Isabella, unaware of the town's growing apprehension, carried herself with an air of grace that intrigued Victor. As their eyes met across the crowded square, a connection sparked, setting into motion a series of events that would forever alter the fate of Ravenshade.

Victor, compelled by an unfamiliar yearning, found himself drawn to Isabella like a moth to a flame. He watched her from the shadows, a silent observer of her daily life. Isabella, in turn, couldn't shake the feeling of being watched, an unsettling sensation that sent shivers down her spine.

Their paths eventually crossed during a chance encounter at the local bookstore. Isabella, browsing the shelves of worn paperbacks, felt a sudden chill in the air. She turned to find Victor standing there, his dark eyes locked onto hers. The air crackled with an unspoken energy—an inexplicable connection that transcended the ordinary.

As Isabella and Victor exchanged pleasantries, an undeniable chemistry simmered beneath the surface. It was a dance of words and glances, each moment charged with an unspoken tension. Isabella, though initially wary of the enigmatic funeral director, felt a strange pull toward him that she couldn't ignore.

Their interactions became a secret affair, hidden from the prying eyes of the town. Isabella found herself entangled in a web of emotions she couldn't comprehend—a fascination with the mysterious man who seemed to straddle the line between the living and the dead.

As their connection deepened, Isabella's presence became a source of solace for Victor, a flicker of light in his shadowy existence. But the townspeople, already on edge, began to take notice of the budding relationship. Whispers spread like wildfire, casting a darker shadow over the couple.

The air in Ravenshade crackled with a palpable tension—a brewing storm of fear, love, and uncertainty. Isabella and Victor, entangled in a love that defied the boundaries of the known, would soon find themselves at the center of a tempest that threatened to tear the fabric of their reality apart. Little did they know that the threads of their fate were intricately woven with the ominous mysteries lurking in the shadows of Ravenshade.

Chapter 4: Forbidden Desires

In the heart of Ravenshade, where the shadows clung to every corner and the air crackled with an unspoken tension, the forbidden romance between Isabella and Victor unfolded. As their connection deepened, the town's apprehension grew, like a storm gathering strength on the horizon.

Isabella, with her radiant smile and gentle spirit, found herself captivated by Victor's enigmatic charm. His eyes, once cold and distant, now softened in her presence. They stole moments together in the moonlit gardens, where whispers of their love danced with the rustling leaves.

But love in Ravenshade was a perilous endeavor, and the couple couldn't escape the watchful eyes of the townspeople. Rumors of their entanglement spread through the community like wildfire, fueled by the fear that clung to the air. Gossip became a weapon, and the couple found themselves at the center of a storm they had not anticipated.

As the town's anxiety mounted, Isabella and Victor faced a growing chorus of disapproval. Friends turned strangers, and neighbors exchanged wary glances whenever the couple passed by. The air, once thick with the scent of blooming flowers, now carried the acrid undertone of fear.

Isabella, torn between her growing love for Victor and the disapproval of the town, found herself caught in a web of conflicting emotions. Victor, haunted by the specter of his own dark secrets, grappled with the weight of bringing danger to the woman he had come to cherish.

One fateful night, as a tempest brewed overhead, Isabella and Victor sought refuge in the mansion's dimly lit halls. The thunder roared, drowning out the distant murmurs of the townspeople. It was a night where passion and fear collided—a night that would shape the destiny of Ravenshade.

In the shadows of the mansion, with the storm raging outside, Isabella confronted Victor about the whispers that had reached her ears. The accusations of his involvement in the mysterious deaths that haunted the town. Victor, his gaze haunted by a thousand regrets, revealed a truth that sent shivers down Isabella's spine.

He was not just a man; he was something else—something that existed in the liminal space between life and death. A creature cursed with an insatiable thirst for human blood. Isabella, torn between terror and love, grappled with the revelation, her heart pounding like a drum in the dark.

As the storm raged on, Isabella made a choice that defied reason. Instead of recoiling in horror, she embraced Victor, vowing to stand by his side against the encroaching darkness. Their love became a beacon, a fragile flame flickering in the face of a malevolent force that sought to tear them apart.

Little did they know, their decision to confront the truth together would set in motion a series of events that would test the limits of their love and the strength of their resolve. The storm outside mirrored the tempest within Ravenshade—a town on the brink of unraveling, where forbidden desires collided with the harsh reality of a world haunted by the unknown.

Chapter 5: A Series of Murders

In the aftermath of the stormy night that had forever changed Isabella and Victor, Ravenshade plunged into a deeper darkness. The air became charged with an oppressive heaviness, and the town's once-familiar streets felt like a labyrinth of uncertainty.

As whispers of the forbidden love between Isabella and Victor lingered, a more ominous shadow fell upon Ravenshade—a series of mysterious deaths that sent shockwaves through the community. The victims, one by one, met their demise in ways that left the townspeople trembling with fear and suspicion.

The first death, that of old Mr. Jenkins, a kind soul who had lived in Ravenshade for decades, occurred under circumstances that defied explanation. His lifeless body, drained of color, was discovered in his home. The air carried a scent of decay, and the townspeople exchanged fearful glances, realizing that something unnatural had occurred.

The second victim, a young florist named Emily, met a similar fate. Her body was found in the moonlit cemetery, surrounded by wilting flowers and an eerie silence that seemed to echo with the weight of the unknown. Fear tightened its grip on Ravenshade, and rumors of a malevolent force grew louder.

The third death struck even closer to home. Mary, the baker known for her warm heart and delicious pastries, was found lifeless in her kitchen. The once-pleasant aroma of freshly baked bread now mingled with the stench of death. Panic spread through the town like wildfire, as the realization set in that a serial killer—or something far more sinister—stalked the streets of Ravenshade.

Detective Martin Harris, a seasoned investigator with a gruff exterior, took charge of the case. The murders, with their inexplicable nature, fueled his determination to bring the killer to justice. As he delved into the investigation, Detective Harris couldn't ignore the undercurrent of fear that permeated the once-peaceful town.

Victor, with his unsettling connection to the funeral home and the recent revelation of his vampiric nature, became a person of interest in the detective's eyes. The townspeople, gripped by paranoia, pointed accusatory fingers at the mysterious funeral director, further intensifying the atmosphere of dread.

Isabella, torn between her love for Victor and the mounting fear gripping the town, found herself entangled in a web of conflicting emotions. She witnessed the accusatory glares and heard the hushed whispers that painted Victor as the perpetrator. Yet, her heart refused to accept the possibility that the man she loved could be capable of such horrors.

As the body count rose, the town's collective anxiety reached a fever pitch. Every creaking floorboard and rustling leaf became a harbinger of doom, and the once-cozy streets now felt like a haunting maze. Ravenshade, once a haven of community, had become a place of fear, suspicion, and unspeakable horrors.

In the face of the escalating nightmare, Isabella and Victor found themselves standing at the crossroads of love and terror. As Detective Harris closed in on the truth, the couple realized that time was running out. They had to confront the malevolent force that haunted Ravenshade, unravel the mysteries that bound them, and somehow find a way to stop the relentless tide of death that threatened to drown the town in darkness.

Chapter 6: The Detective's Hunch

Ravenshade, gripped by the grim specter of a series of mysterious deaths, became a town shrouded in fear. The once-familiar streets now echoed with the hushed whispers of its frightened inhabitants. Detective Martin Harris, a weathered figure with a determination etched into the lines of his face, found himself thrust into a case that defied rational explanation.

The first murder, that of Mr. Jenkins, had left a haunting imprint on Detective Harris. As he examined the scene, a gnawing unease settled in the pit of his stomach. The lack of discernible motive and the eerie circumstances surrounding the deaths were like pieces of a puzzle that refused to fit together.

The detective, known for his pragmatic approach, couldn't shake the feeling that there was more to these murders than met the eye. Each crime scene bore a sinister signature—a peculiar arrangement of shadows, an inexplicable coldness, and an air thick with the stench of death. As he delved deeper into the investigation, Detective Harris sensed that he was treading on the edge of something far beyond the scope of his understanding.

The townspeople, already on edge from the string of deaths, cast wary glances at each other. Whispers of a malevolent force lurking in the shadows spread through Ravenshade like wildfire. The once-cohesive community now teetered on the brink of paranoia, and the detective became acutely aware of the fear that pulsed through the town's veins.

Victor Blackwood, the mysterious funeral director, had become a person of interest in Detective Harris's investigation. The townspeople, driven by a collective hysteria, pointed accusatory fingers at the enigmatic figure who had taken residence on the outskirts of town. The detective, skeptical but compelled by the mounting evidence, began to scrutinize Victor's every move.

As Detective Harris questioned Victor and probed the funeral home's secrets, a chilling revelation emerged—the connection between the deaths and the eerie occurrences at the mansion. The detective's hunch intensified, and a grim suspicion crept into his mind. Could Victor Blackwood be more than just a bystander in this macabre puzzle?

Isabella, caught between her love for Victor and the rising tide of suspicion, found herself torn. The detective's inquiries cast a shadow over the fragile sanctuary she had built with Victor. The town, gripped by fear, watched the unfolding drama with bated breath.

Detective Harris, driven by an unrelenting determination to uncover the truth, became haunted by dreams that blurred the line between reality and nightmare. Visions of shadowy figures and blood-stained corridors tormented his nights, leaving him on edge during waking hours. The once-sturdy detective felt the tendrils of an unseen force wrapping around him, urging him to unveil the malevolence that lurked beneath Ravenshade's surface.

The investigation took a darker turn when Emily, the young florist, became the latest victim. The townspeople, now consumed by panic, demanded swift justice. The detective, fueled by a sense of urgency, intensified his scrutiny of Victor Blackwood. Every piece of evidence, every sidelong glance, and every cryptic detail pointed toward the funeral director as the epicenter of the town's descent into madness.

As Detective Harris closed in on Victor, Isabella and her beloved found themselves caught in the eye of the storm. The town, torn between fear and a desperate need for answers, stood on the precipice of a revelation that would either shatter the illusions of normalcy or plunge Ravenshade into an abyss of eternal darkness. The detective's hunch, though fraught with uncertainty, had become a relentless force propelling him toward a confrontation that would test the limits of his convictions and unveil the true horrors that lurked in the shadows of Ravenshade.

Chapter 7: Love Blossoms

In the looming shadow of Detective Harris's intensifying investigation, Ravenshade became a town gripped not only by fear but also by the blossoming tendrils of forbidden love. Isabella and

Victor, entangled in a romance that defied reason, found solace in each other's arms amidst the encroaching darkness.

As the detective continued to scrutinize Victor's every move, the couple sought refuge in the sanctuary of the mansion. The walls, though adorned with ornate tapestries, seemed to whisper secrets of the ancient darkness that lurked within. Isabella and Victor, in the quiet moments stolen from the town's judgmental gaze, found a fragile oasis where love could flourish despite the gathering storm.

The mansion's gardens, once vibrant with life, became a clandestine meeting place for the couple. Flowers bloomed in hues of blood-red and midnight black, mirroring the intensity of their emotions. The moon, a silent witness to their clandestine meetings, bathed the lovers in its soft glow as they exchanged vows of devotion and faced the uncertainties that loomed over Ravenshade.

Yet, even in the refuge of their love, the town's suspicion cast a long, chilling shadow. Isabella, torn between her loyalty to Victor and the fear of losing him, faced the challenge of shielding their love from the prying eyes of the townspeople. The once-familiar faces now bore expressions of judgment, and the couple's stolen moments became increasingly fraught with the looming threat of exposure.

Detective Harris, driven by an unrelenting determination to solve the baffling murders, grew ever closer to unraveling the secrets that the mansion held. Every visit to Victor's funeral home yielded more questions than answers, and the detective couldn't shake the feeling that he was on the verge of a revelation that would shake Ravenshade to its core.

Isabella, caught in the crossfire of love and fear, became the emotional fulcrum upon which the town's destiny teetered. Her heart, entwined with Victor's, bore the weight of secrets that threatened to unravel everything they held dear. The mansion, once a symbol of Victor's mysterious allure, now became a crucible where love and darkness collided.

The townspeople, fueled by a collective paranoia that mirrored Detective Harris's suspicions, began to rally against the perceived threat that Victor posed. An air of tension gripped the once-cohesive community, and the streets buzzed with speculative murmurs. The fear, palpable in the air, manifested as accusatory glances and hushed conversations that painted Victor Blackwood as the embodiment of the town's deepest nightmares.

As the couple faced the mounting pressure from all sides, their love deepened into a bond that transcended the mortal coil. Isabella, despite the chaos that surrounded them, stood steadfast beside Victor. The funeral director, haunted by the weight of his own existence, found solace in the warmth of Isabella's unwavering love.

But love in Ravenshade, tainted by the fear of the unknown, became a fragile thread that threatened to snap under the strain. The mansion, once a refuge, now echoed with the footsteps of impending doom. The town, on the brink of collective hysteria, stood at the crossroads of love and horror, where the choices made by Isabella and Victor would determine not only their fate but the fate of Ravenshade itself. As Detective Harris closed in on the truth, the lovers clung to each other, hoping that their love could withstand the tempest that raged within and beyond the haunted walls of the mansion.

Chapter 8: The Vampire's Dilemma

As the moon cast an eerie glow over Ravenshade, the town teetered on the precipice of dread. Detective Harris's investigation, fueled by a relentless determination to unearth the truth, cast a long shadow over Victor Blackwood and the forbidden love he shared with Isabella. In the mansion on the outskirts, where the air hummed with ancient secrets, the vampire faced an internal dilemma that threatened to unravel the fragile tapestry of his existence.

Victor, haunted by the specter of his own nature, grappled with the burden of his insatiable thirst for human blood. The once-cold eyes that had softened in Isabella's presence now reflected the torment within. The mansion, with its twisting corridors and dimly lit chambers, became a prison of conflicting desires—an eternal struggle between the man who longed for love and the creature that craved the darkness.

Isabella, sensing the turmoil that consumed Victor, became a steadfast pillar of support. Their love, though tested by the town's suspicions and the detective's relentless pursuit, held a fragility that transcended the mortal realm. But the vampire's dilemma cast a looming shadow over their moments of stolen tenderness.

As Detective Harris unearthed more clues that pointed towards Victor's involvement in the mysterious deaths, the town's paranoia escalated. Whispers of dark rituals and malevolent forces echoed through the streets, painting the funeral director as the harbinger of doom. The once-thriving community now stood at the brink of collective hysteria, with fear coiling around every corner like a venomous serpent.

Victor, burdened by the weight of his existence, confided in Isabella about the curse that bound him—a curse that demanded the lifeblood of the living. The revelation sent shockwaves through her, and the couple found themselves entangled in a love that transcended the boundaries of mortality. Isabella, torn between the man she loved and the monstrous truth he harbored, faced a choice that would shape the destiny of Ravenshade.

The mansion's walls, adorned with portraits of faces long lost to time, seemed to echo with the agonized whispers of the undead. Victor, desperate to find a way to quell his bloodlust and protect the woman he loved, delved into forbidden tomes and ancient scrolls. The library, a repository of arcane knowledge, held the key to a solution that could either free Victor from his vampiric chains or condemn him to an eternity of darkness.

Detective Harris, unaware of the supernatural forces at play, closed in on the funeral home with a determination that mirrored the inexorable march of fate. The evidence, though circumstantial, pointed towards Victor as the elusive thread connecting the deaths that plagued Ravenshade. The town, perched on the precipice of hysteria, clamored for justice as the vampire's dilemma deepened.

Isabella, caught between the detective's relentless pursuit and Victor's struggle for redemption, became the emotional fulcrum upon which the fate of Ravenshade swayed. The couple, united by a love that defied reason, faced a race against time to unravel the mysteries that bound them and find a way to quench the insatiable thirst that threatened to consume Victor's soul.

As the mansion's chambers echoed with the whispered incantations of forgotten lore, and the detective closed in on the truth, the vampire's dilemma intensified. The town, unaware of the supernatural forces that governed their destinies, stood on the brink of revelation. In the heart of Ravenshade, where love and horror danced a macabre waltz, the choices made by Isabella, Victor, and Detective Harris would determine whether the town would succumb to the shadows or find a glimmer of salvation in the midst of the encroaching darkness.

Chapter 9: The Investigation Heats Up

Ravenshade, enveloped in a shroud of fear and suspicion, felt the town's heartbeat quicken as Detective Martin Harris intensified his pursuit of the truth. The series of mysterious deaths, the forbidden love between Isabella and Victor, and the looming presence of an ancient darkness cast a pall over the community. As Detective Harris delved deeper into the investigation, the air became thick with tension, and the town's collective anxiety reached a fevered pitch.

The detective, driven by an unyielding determination to solve the baffling murders, sifted through the clues like a bloodhound on the scent. Every visit to Victor's funeral home unearthed more questions than answers, and the whispers that painted the enigmatic funeral director as the harbinger of doom grew louder. The once-cohesive community now stood divided, with suspicions tearing through the fabric of trust that had bound Ravenshade together.

Isabella, torn between her love for Victor and the detective's relentless pursuit, found herself caught in a whirlwind of conflicting emotions. The mansion, once a sanctuary, now echoed with the haunting whispers of secrets long buried. The town's scrutiny intensified

Chapter 10 Unraveling Secrets

The darkness clung to Ravenshade like a malevolsent force as Detective Martin Harris pressed on with his investigation, fueled by an unyielding determination to untangle the web of mysteries that gripped the town. The air crackled with tension, and the once-close-knit community now stood on the precipice of revelation.

Detective Harris, armed with the fragments of evidence he had gathered, delved into the funeral home's murky secrets. The flickering candles, the ominous undertones, and the whispers of forbidden rituals painted Victor Blackwood as a figure of suspicion. As the detective sifted through the shadows, the walls seemed to close in around him, whispering secrets that sent shivers down his spine.

Isabella, caught in the crossfire of the investigation, felt the weight of the town's gaze bearing down on her. The once-hidden love between her and Victor now stood exposed, a fragile flame flickering against the encroaching darkness. The mansion's halls, once a sanctuary for their stolen moments, echoed with the haunting footsteps of Detective Harris, each stride bringing them closer to the heart of the mysteries that bound Ravenshade.

Victor, tormented by his dual nature, grappled with the knowledge that his very existence was a threat to the town and the woman he loved. The library, a repository of forbidden knowledge, beckoned him to seek a solution that would sever the ties between his vampiric curse and the string of deaths that haunted Ravenshade.

As Detective Harris followed the trail of clues, the town's paranoia heightened. Whispers of curses, supernatural entities, and the malevolent influence of the funeral director spread like wildfire. The once-thriving streets now bore the weight of fear, and the townspeople exchanged furtive glances as shadows played tricks on their senses.

Isabella, in her desperate attempt to shield Victor from the detective's scrutiny, sought answers within the mansion's ancient tomes. The pages, filled with cryptic symbols and arcane incantations, hinted at a dark history that transcended time. With each revelation, the couple's love became a beacon in the gathering storm, a flicker of hope against the encroaching night.

Detective Harris, unbeknownst to him, stood at the threshold of the mansion's secrets. The detective's hunch, driven by a relentless pursuit of justice, led him to confront Victor in the dimly lit chambers where the air seemed to vibrate with suppressed power. Isabella, torn between her loyalty to Victor and the looming threat of exposure, stood on the precipice of a revelation that could shatter the fragile peace that remained in Ravenshade.

The mansion, a silent witness to the unfolding drama, held the key to the town's salvation or damnation. The detective's footsteps echoed through the corridors, each one carrying the weight of impending confrontation. As the secrets of Ravenshade's dark tapestry unraveled, the town stood on the edge of a precipice, where the choices made in the coming moments would determine the destiny of its inhabitants and the fate of the love that dared to bloom in the face of an ancient, malevolent force.

Chapter 11: Confrontation in the Shadows

Ravenshade, a town gripped by fear and secrets, found itself at a pivotal moment as Detective Martin Harris closed in on the enigma that was Victor Blackwood. The detective's footsteps echoed through the dimly lit corridors of the mansion, and the air seemed to hum with the weight of impending revelation. Isabella, torn between her love for Victor and the looming confrontation, felt the town's destiny hang in the balance.

Detective Harris, fueled by the fragments of evidence and the relentless pursuit of justice, approached Victor in the heart of the mansion. The funeral director, his eyes reflecting the torment within, awaited the inevitable confrontation. The room felt charged with an otherworldly energy as the detective, unaware of the supernatural forces at play, prepared to unveil the mysteries that had cast a shadow over Ravenshade.

Isabella, standing at the intersection of love and dread, watched as the two figures faced each other. The detective's accusing gaze met Victor's haunted eyes, and in that moment, the mansion's walls seemed to pulse with an ancient heartbeat. The air crackled with tension as the detective began to question Victor about the deaths that haunted the town.

Victor, caught between the weight of his vampiric nature and the desire to protect Isabella, felt the walls closing in around him. The detective's questions were a relentless assault, each inquiry tearing at the fragile facade that concealed the dark truths within. Isabella, unable to bear the strain, clutched the edges of her reality, her heart pounding with a rhythm that echoed through the mansion.

As the confrontation unfolded, the shadows themselves seemed to dance with malevolence. Whispers of forgotten curses and the thirst for blood intertwined with the detective's accusations, creating a symphony of dread that reverberated through the once-hallowed halls. The mansion, a repository of ancient secrets, bore witness to a clash between mortal justice and the supernatural forces that lurked within.

In the midst of the confrontation, Isabella, desperate to shield Victor, revealed the depths of their forbidden love. The confession hung in the air, a revelation that added another layer to the town's collective horror. The detective, now entangled in a web of love and darkness, grappled with the realization that the enigmatic funeral director was not merely a suspect but a creature torn between worlds.

The town, oblivious to the supernatural drama unfolding, trembled on the brink of chaos. The whispers of a malevolent force echoed through the streets, and the air seemed to thicken with an unspoken dread. The choices made in the mansion's dimly lit chambers would ripple through Ravenshade, shaping its fate and the destinies of those entwined in the macabre tapestry of love and horror.

As the confrontation reached its climax, the mansion's secrets threatened to spill into the town's consciousness like a tidal wave of revelation. Isabella, Victor, and Detective Harris stood at the epicenter of a storm that would either consume Ravenshade in darkness or expose the truth that had long languished in the shadows. The drama that unfolded within those walls would leave an indelible mark on the town, forever altering the course of its history.

Chapter 12: The Pact of Shadows

The revelation of Victor's vampiric nature and Isabella's forbidden love had plunged Ravenshade into a maelstrom of horror and uncertainty. Detective Martin Harris, still grappling with the supernatural truth, stood at the crossroads of mortal justice and the ancient darkness that clung to the town. As the trio confronted the secrets within the mansion's walls, the air pulsed with an ominous energy, foretelling a climax that would resonate through Ravenshade's very soul.

The detective, eyes wide with disbelief, demanded answers from Victor. The funeral director, his features etched with a mixture of guilt and defiance, hesitated before weaving a tale of curses, immortal thirst, and centuries-old shadows. Isabella, her heart pounding in rhythm with the town's collective fear, pleaded for understanding as the revelations unfolded like a nightmarish tapestry.

Within the dimly lit chambers, the mansion seemed to rebel against the weight of its own secrets. Shadows danced with an eerie sentience, contorting into shapes that whispered forgotten horrors. The detective's interrogation became a dance with the unknown, each revelation more horrifying than the last. The very fabric of reality seemed to fray as the trio navigated the treacherous terrain between the living and the undead.

As Victor recounted his cursed existence, the detective's skepticism clashed with the supernatural truths that defied logic. Isabella, caught in the crossfire, felt the tension escalate like a storm on the horizon. The mansion, a silent witness to centuries of secrets, bore witness to the fragility of mortal understanding in the face of immortal mysteries.

In the shadows, an ancient force stirred—a malevolence that transcended time and clung to Victor like a symbiotic curse. The town, unaware of the supernatural tempest that raged within the mansion, trembled on the brink of a revelation that would either shatter the illusions of normalcy or plunge it into an abyss of eternal darkness.

As the detective continued his relentless pursuit of truth, Isabella and Victor faced a dilemma that mirrored the town's uncertainty. Could the vampire's insatiable thirst for blood be quenched, and was redemption possible for a creature that had straddled the line between life and death for centuries? The answers, buried in the cryptic tomes of the mansion's library, eluded them like elusive specters.

The air within Ravenshade became charged with an unspoken pact—a covenant between shadows and the living. The mansion's secrets, once bound by the veils of time, threatened to rupture the fragile balance between the mundane and the supernatural. Isabella, Victor, and Detective Harris stood at the nexus of this cosmic struggle, each choice echoing through the town like a tolling bell.

As the confrontation neared its climax, the mansion's halls seemed to close in, trapping the trio in a labyrinth of revelations and uncertainty. The choices made within those walls would determine not only the fate of Victor and Isabella but also the destiny of Ravenshade itself. In the heart of the macabre drama, where love and horror danced an intricate waltz, the town stood on the brink of a revelation that would either herald salvation or plunge it into an abyss of eternal night.

Chapter 13: A Pact with Darkness

The air within Ravenshade remained thick with tension as the revelation of Victor's vampiric nature unfolded in the dimly lit chambers of the mansion. Detective Martin Harris, still grappling with the unearthly truth, found himself caught between the pursuit of justice and the incomprehensible horrors that seemed to weave themselves into the fabric of the town. Isabella and Victor, entwined in a love that defied the boundaries of mortality, stood at the epicenter of a cosmic struggle that threatened to consume them all.

As the detective pressed Victor for more details, the funeral director spoke of an ancient curse that bound him to the shadows—a curse that demanded the lifeblood of the living. Isabella, her heart heavy with the weight of forbidden love and supernatural revelations, pleaded for understanding. The mansion, a repository of arcane knowledge, seemed to echo with the collective gasp of a town on the brink of unraveling.

The detective's skepticism clashed with the supernatural truths that defied reason. The very foundation of reality trembled as Victor's tale unfolded like a sinister lullaby. In the flickering candlelight, the shadows contorted into grotesque shapes, mirroring the torment within the immortal being who stood at the center of the unfolding drama.

As the trio navigated the labyrinth of revelations, an ancient force stirred in the shadows—a malevolence that had haunted Ravenshade for centuries. The mansion, a silent witness to a pact with darkness, seemed to breathe with a sentience that transcended time. Isabella, Victor, and the detective stood at the threshold of a cosmic reckoning, where the choices made would resonate through the town's very soul.

Isabella, torn between her love for Victor and the fear that gripped the town, sought answers within the dusty tomes of the mansion's library. The pages whispered of forbidden rituals, of curses that transcended generations, and of a way to sever the ties that bound Victor to the insatiable thirst for blood. The library, once a haven of knowledge, now felt like a portal to the abyss.

Detective Harris, his mind a battleground of rationality and supernatural revelation, grappled with the notion that the creature standing before him was more than a suspect—it was a force that defied the laws of nature. The detective's resolve wavered as the walls seemed to close in, each revelation pulling him deeper into the abyss of the unknown.

As the tension reached its zenith, a pact with darkness emerged—an unspoken agreement between the living and the undead. The mansion's ancient secrets threatened to spill into the town like a cascade of shadows, challenging the fragile equilibrium that had masked the supernatural truths for centuries.

In the heart of Ravenshade, where mortal and immortal forces collided, Isabella, Victor, and Detective Harris faced a choice that would shape the destiny of the town. The air crackled with an otherworldly energy as they grappled with the implications of the revelations. The mansion's chambers, once a sanctuary, now felt like a crucible where the town's fate would be forged in the fires of an ancient, malevolent force.

As the trio stood at the crossroads of love and horror, the town held its breath, unaware of the cosmic drama that played out within the haunted walls of the mansion. The choices made within those dimly lit chambers would echo through Ravenshade's history, determining whether the town would succumb to the encroaching darkness or find a glimmer of salvation in the midst of the supernatural storm.

Chapter 14: Veil of Shadows Unveiled

The revelation of Victor's vampiric nature had plunged Ravenshade into a maelstrom of fear and uncertainty. The town, once shrouded in a deceptive sense of normalcy, now stood at the precipice of an abyss, where the supernatural and mortal collided in a cosmic dance of dread. As Isabella, Victor, and Detective Martin Harris grappled with the unfolding horrors within the mansion, the air vibrated with an otherworldly tension.

Victor, haunted by the weight of his immortal existence, stood as a living paradox—a creature of the night who longed for the warmth of love. Isabella, torn between loyalty to her beloved and the looming threat that Victor posed to the town, felt the burden of an impossible choice. Detective Harris, caught in the crossfire of supernatural revelation and mortal duty, stood as a lone bastion against the encroaching darkness.

Within the dimly lit chambers, the trio confronted the ancient force that stirred in the shadows. Victor, his eyes reflecting centuries of torment, spoke of a pact with darkness—a curse that bound him to an insatiable thirst for human blood. The detective, though still grappling with disbelief, felt the weight of supernatural truths closing in like a vice.

As Isabella sought answers within the dusty tomes of the mansion's library, the pages revealed a path to redemption. Whispers of ancient rituals and forgotten incantations hinted at a way to sever the vampiric curse that gripped Victor's soul. The library, a repository of secrets, became a battleground where the forces of salvation and damnation clashed.

The mansion itself seemed alive with the echoes of centuries gone by. The walls pulsed with an otherworldly energy, and the very air seemed to breathe with sentience. Shadows danced with malevolence, contorting into nightmarish shapes that mirrored the internal struggles of those within. The choices made within those walls would reverberate through the town's history.

Detective Harris, torn between the pursuit of justice and the supernatural revelations that defied reason, faced a test of resolve. The evidence of Victor's vampiric nature seemed irrefutable, yet the detective grappled with the knowledge that the town stood on the brink of a truth that transcended mortal understanding.

Isabella, armed with the newfound knowledge from the ancient tomes, confronted Victor with the possibility of breaking the curse. The mansion's chambers became a crucible where love and redemption clashed with the ancient malevolence that lurked in the shadows. The choices made by the trio would determine whether Ravenshade would be condemned to eternal night or find a glimmer of hope amidst the encroaching darkness.

As the confrontation reached its climax, the mansion's secrets threatened to spill into the town's consciousness. The very foundation of reality trembled, and Ravenshade stood at the crossroads of salvation and damnation. Isabella, Victor, and Detective Harris faced a cosmic reckoning, their fates intertwined with the town's destiny in ways they could not yet comprehend.

The air crackled with an intensity that mirrored the town's collective fear. In the heart of Ravenshade, where love and horror had become inseparable, the trio prepared to make a final stand against the ancient force that sought to claim their souls. The choices made within those haunted walls would echo through eternity, sealing the town's fate in a veil of shadows that veiled the truth in mystery and dread.

Chapter 15: The Descent into Darkness

Ravenshade, now ensnared in a web of unearthly revelations, stood on the precipice of a descent into the unknown. As Isabella, Victor, and Detective Martin Harris grappled with the implications of the vampiric curse and the potential for redemption, the town's pulse quickened with a shared fear that hung in the air like a looming storm. The mansion, a crucible of love, horror, and ancient malevolence, became the stage for a final act that would determine Ravenshade's destiny.

Isabella, armed with the esoteric knowledge gleaned from the mansion's library, shared her findings with Victor. The ritual to break the curse loomed before them, a glimmer of hope in the encroaching darkness. Detective Harris, torn between skepticism and the undeniable supernatural truths, stood witness to a cosmic struggle that transcended the bounds of mortal understanding.

The trio, bound by fate and the choices that lay ahead, entered the mansion's ritual chamber. Candles flickered ominously, casting dancing shadows that seemed to whisper of the ancient forces at play. The air hummed with an eerie energy as the town's destiny unfolded within those dimly lit walls.

Victor, the weight of centuries etched on his features, faced the ritual with a mixture of desperation and determination. Isabella, torn between love and the fear of what Victor might become, stood steadfast at his side. Detective Harris, though still skeptical, sensed the gravity of the moment—a moment that could tip the scales between salvation and damnation.

As the ritual began, the mansion seemed to come alive with an unseen force. Shadows writhed and contorted, casting grotesque silhouettes on the chamber walls. The town, unaware of the supernatural drama unfolding, felt an unspoken unease that permeated the very fabric of Ravenshade.

The ritual's incantations echoed through the chamber, and the air became charged with an otherworldly tension. Isabella's voice, trembling yet resolute, mingled with the supernatural whispers that seemed to seep from the very stones of the mansion. The detective, caught in the crossfire of ancient forces, could feel the town's fate hanging in the balance.

As the ritual reached its crescendo, a palpable darkness descended upon the chamber. Victor, his features contorted in pain, bore the weight of the ritual's transformative power. Isabella, her heart pounding with a mixture of hope and fear, clung to the belief that love could conquer even the darkest curses.

Suddenly, an otherworldly scream pierced the air—a sound that seemed to echo through the ages. The mansion's walls shook, and the very ground beneath Ravenshade quivered. The town, now aware of an unseen turmoil, stood on the edge of collective hysteria.

Isabella, her eyes fixed on Victor, witnessed a transformation that defied the laws of nature. The ritual's outcome remained uncertain, and the shadows that clung to the chamber seemed to pulse with an ancient malevolence. Detective Harris, his skepticism waning in the face of the supernatural spectacle, felt the weight of the town's fear pressing down upon him.

In the heart of Ravenshade, where mortal and immortal forces clashed in a final, dramatic confrontation, the choices made within the ritual chamber would determine the town's fate. The air crackled with an intensity that mirrored the collective pulse of the townspeople, unaware of the battle that raged within the haunted walls of the mansion. As the ritual's echoes reverberated through Ravenshade, the town held its breath, suspended in a moment that would either usher in a new dawn or plunge them into an eternal night.

Chapter 16: Shadows Unleashed

Ravenshade, teetering on the brink of an otherworldly revelation, held its breath as the ritual within the mansion's chamber reached its crescendo. Isabella, Victor, and Detective Martin Harris stood at the epicenter of a cosmic struggle, where love and horror clashed in the dimly lit sanctuary. The air pulsed with an intensity that mirrored the collective fear of a town thrust into the heart of supernatural upheaval.

The ritual's incantations reverberated through the chamber, casting an eerie glow on the faces of those entwined in its mystical dance. Isabella, her voice intermingling with the arcane whispers, clung to the belief that the ritual could sever Victor's vampiric curse. The detective, his skepticism eroding in the face of the unfolding spectacle, sensed the town's fate hanging in the balance.

As the ritual's power surged, the mansion seemed to come alive with an unseen force. Shadows, once confined to the corners, writhed and contorted like malevolent specters. The very foundation of the town trembled, and an unspoken unease settled over Ravenshade like a shroud of impending doom.

Victor, caught in the throes of transformation, emitted an otherworldly scream that seemed to pierce the veil between the mortal and the supernatural. Isabella, her heart wrenching at the sight of his torment, clutched onto hope as the ritual's arcane energies wove through the fabric of his being. The detective, torn between duty and the supernatural forces at play, could feel the town's collective anxiety pressing upon him like a weight.

Suddenly, the chamber erupted in a burst of blinding light—a radiance that seemed to defy the oppressive darkness that had haunted Ravenshade. The town, now aware of an unseen turmoil, stood on the brink of collective hysteria as the mansion's ancient secrets threatened to spill into the streets.

As the light subsided, the chamber fell into an eerie stillness. Isabella's eyes, wide with anticipation, sought Victor amidst the lingering shadows. The detective, bracing for the unknown, felt the weight of the town's destiny pressing upon him like an insurmountable burden.

Victor emerged from the ritual's aftermath, his features transformed but free from the vampiric pallor that had defined him for centuries. Isabella, a mixture of relief and awe in her eyes, rushed to his side. The mansion, still bathed in an otherworldly aura, seemed to exhale a sigh of ancient secrets unveiled.

The town, oblivious to the supernatural drama within the mansion, stood on the cusp of revelation. Isabella, Victor, and Detective Harris emerged from the chamber, their faces etched with the indelible marks of a cosmic confrontation. The air, now thick with uncertainty, carried whispers of change that wafted through Ravenshade's streets like a haunting melody.

Isabella, her hand entwined with Victor's, faced the town that had become a crucible of love and horror. The detective, still grappling with the unearthly truths that defied reason, braced for the aftermath of the ritual. Ravenshade, a town forever altered by the events within the mansion, held its breath as the trio stepped into the unknown, where the shadows of the past had been unleashed, and the future hung in the delicate balance between light and darkness.

Chapter 17: Echoes of Redemption

The aftermath of the ritual lingered over Ravenshade like a ghostly apparition, casting an unsettling stillness over the town. Isabella, Victor, and Detective Martin Harris emerged from the mansion's chamber, their faces a tapestry of emotions. The air crackled with an unspoken tension, and the town stood on the edge of a revelation that pulsed through the very heart of Ravenshade.

Isabella, her hand tightly clasped with Victor's, faced the wary gazes of the townspeople. The couple, now transformed by the ritual's mysterious energies, became a living enigma in the eyes of those who had only glimpsed the shadows of their secrets. Detective Harris, still grappling with the supernatural truths that defied his rational mind, observed the unfolding drama with a sense of trepidation.

Ravenshade, oblivious to the cosmic struggle that had played out within the mansion, felt the lingering echoes of change. Whispers of the ritual's aftermath spread through the streets, like an invisible current carrying tales of redemption and supernatural forces transcending mortal understanding. The town, once cocooned in the familiarity of everyday life, now stood at the crossroads of normalcy and the unknown.

Isabella, sensing the town's collective gaze, stood firm. The love between her and Victor, now freed from the vampiric curse, became a beacon in the encroaching darkness. The mansion, once a harbinger of fear, now held the promise of redemption—an enigma that the townspeople could neither comprehend nor ignore.

Detective Harris, torn between duty and the supernatural truths he had witnessed, felt the weight of the town's uncertainty pressing upon him. The evidence of the ritual's transformative power stood before him, challenging the very foundations of his understanding of the world. The detective, haunted by the shadows of the unknown, braced for the inevitable questions that would cascade through Ravenshade like a tidal wave.

As the trio ventured into the town's heart, they encountered curious glances and hushed conversations. The air seemed to thicken with a palpable tension as the townspeople grappled with the implications of the supernatural events that had unfolded within the mansion. Ravenshade, a town steeped in ancient secrets, now faced a reckoning that would shape its destiny.

Isabella, guided by a newfound strength, addressed the townspeople. She spoke of redemption, of breaking the shackles of ancient curses, and of the transformative power of love. The mansion, once a symbol of fear, became a testament to the resilience of the human spirit against the encroaching shadows.

The detective, though still skeptical, sensed the sincerity in Isabella's words. The town, caught between fear and the allure of redemption, stood at the precipice of a collective decision. As Isabella and Victor's love became a rallying point, the streets of Ravenshade echoed with a chorus of uncertainty and anticipation.

The mansion, bathed in the glow of newfound hope, stood as a silent witness to the town's transformation. The shadows that had haunted its corridors for centuries seemed to retreat, leaving behind the echoes of an ancient struggle that had reached its climax. Ravenshade, a town forever changed, faced a future that bore the indelible marks of a cosmic drama that had played out within its very heart.

As the trio navigated the streets, they became unwitting symbols of a supernatural redemption that defied the expectations of mortal understanding. The town, now poised between skepticism and the allure of a new beginning, grappled with the aftermath of the ritual that had unraveled the tapestry of its secrets. In the heart of Ravenshade, where love and horror had danced a macabre waltz, the choices made by Isabella, Victor, and Detective Harris would ripple through the town's history, shaping its future in the lingering echoes of redemption.

Chapter 18: Unveiling the Abyss

The aftermath of the ritual lingered over Ravenshade like a ghostly mist, leaving the town caught between the allure of redemption and the ever-present shadows of uncertainty. Isabella,

Victor, and Detective Martin Harris became unwitting symbols of a supernatural transformation that defied the logic of everyday life. The air crackled with an unspoken tension, and the town stood on the precipice of revelation, unsure of what lay beyond the veils of the unknown.

Isabella, her hand still entwined with Victor's, faced the wary gazes of the townspeople. The couple, marked by the aftermath of the ritual, became an enigma that both fascinated and frightened the community. Detective Harris, still grappling with the supernatural truths that had unraveled within the mansion, observed the unfolding drama with a sense of trepidation.

Ravenshade, now privy to the echoes of the ritual's aftermath, buzzed with speculation and fear. Whispers of the transformative power of the ritual spread like wildfire through the streets, conjuring images of redemption and the supernatural forces that had, until now, lurked in the shadows. The town, once shielded by the mundane, now stood exposed to the abyss that yawned beneath the surface.

Isabella, sensing the town's collective gaze, felt the weight of expectation and fear. The love she shared with Victor, now freed from the vampiric curse, became both a beacon and a harbinger of the unknown. The mansion, once a dwelling of fear, now stood as a gateway to the mysteries that Ravenshade had long sought to bury.

Detective Harris, torn between his duty as an officer of the law and the supernatural reality that defied his understanding, grappled with the uncertainty that pervaded the town. The detective, once a bastion of rationality, now stood at the precipice of an abyss that threatened to swallow the very fabric of his beliefs.

As the trio moved through the town, they encountered a mixture of curiosity and trepidation. The air seemed thick with an invisible tension as the townspeople wrestled with the implications of the supernatural events that had unfolded within the mansion.

Ravenshade, a town shackled by ancient secrets, now faced the daunting task of confronting the abyss that had opened within its very heart.

Isabella, guided by a newfound strength, addressed the townspeople once more. She spoke of redemption, of the transformative power of the ritual, and of the love that had defied the darkness. The mansion, now both a symbol of fear and hope, echoed with Isabella's words, and the town listened with a collective sense of awe and trepidation.

The detective, though still skeptical, found himself caught in the undertow of Isabella's sincerity. The town, standing at the crossroads of skepticism and the allure of a new beginning, grappled with the aftermath of the ritual that had unraveled the tapestry of its secrets. Ravenshade, a town forever changed, faced a future that held the indelible marks of a cosmic drama that had played out within its very core.

As the trio moved through the streets, they became reluctant heralds of a supernatural redemption that defied the expectations of the mortal realm. The town, now standing at the brink of an uncertain future, wrestled with the aftermath of the ritual that had laid bare the shadows of its own existence. In the heart of Ravenshade, where love and horror had danced their intricate waltz, the choices made by Isabella, Victor, and Detective Harris would echo through the town's history, leaving behind a legacy that would forever haunt the collective consciousness of the community.

Chapter 19: The Fraying Veil

Ravenshade, once shrouded in mystery, now stood exposed to the aftermath of the transformative ritual. Isabella, Victor, and Detective Martin Harris became both witnesses and participants in a drama that unfolded within the streets and minds of the town. The air vibrated with a sense of uncertainty, as if the fabric hanging precariously on the edge of the unknown.

Isabella, holding Victor's hand tightly, felt the weight of the town's collective gaze. The ritual had changed them, and the town, uncertain of the nature of this transformation, teetered on the edge of fear and fascination. Detective Harris, still grappling with the supernatural truths, sensed the tension that clung to the air like a suffocating mist.

Rumors and whispers about the trio's encounter with the supernatural spread like wildfire through Ravenshade. The streets, once familiar and comforting, now buzzed with an unsettling energy. The townspeople, caught between skepticism and the lingering shadows of the ritual, awaited the next chapter in a story that had unraveled the very fabric of their existence.

Isabella, recognizing the town's need for understanding, decided to address the community once more. Standing in the town square, she spoke of the ritual's purpose, of breaking the shackles of ancient curses, and of love as the guiding force that had brought them to this moment. The mansion, looming in the background, seemed to watch over the unfolding drama, its walls echoing with the secrets that had been laid bare.

Detective Harris, torn between duty and the supernatural forces at play, observed the crowd. The detective, once the embodiment of law and order, now grappled with the unknown, unsure of how to restore a semblance of normalcy to a town caught in the throes of the extraordinary.

As Isabella's words resonated through the square, a sudden chill swept through Ravenshade. The atmosphere thickened, and an oppressive darkness seemed to claw its way into the hearts of the townspeople. Whispers of an ancient malevolence, awakened by the ritual, slithered through the air like a serpent ready to strike.

Unseen by the crowd, shadows gathered at the periphery, forming grotesque shapes that danced in the corners of perception. The town's newfound hope began to waver, and a sense of foreboding settled over Ravenshade like a shroud. The supernatural forces, once thought to be quelled, now threatened to unravel the fragile peace that had briefly settled upon the town.

Isabella, sensing the shift in the atmosphere, felt a knot tighten in her stomach. Victor, by her side, gripped her hand with a newfound intensity. Detective Harris, his instincts tingling with an eerie premonition, scanned the surroundings, searching for the source of the encroaching darkness.

Suddenly, a piercing scream shattered the uneasy calm. A figure emerged from the shadows, distorted and contorted, a manifestation of the malevolence that had been unleashed. The townspeople recoiled in horror as the once-familiar face twisted into a grotesque mask of supernatural malevolence.

Panic spread through the square like wildfire. The fraying veil between the known and the unknown tore open, and the townspeople, once united by curiosity and fear, now scattered in terror. The supernatural forces, emboldened by the disturbance, manifested in eerie shapes that slithered through the streets, leaving a trail of horror in their wake.

Isabella, Victor, and Detective Harris found themselves at the center of a maelstrom. The mansion, once a symbol of redemption, now seemed like a gateway to a realm of nightmares. The trio, burdened by the consequences of the ritual, stood amidst the chaos, grappling with the realization that the forces they had awakened were far more malevolent than they could have ever imagined.

As the shadows tightened their grip on Ravenshade, the town, once again, found itself thrust into a relentless battle between the supernatural and the mundane. The choices made in the aftermath of the ritual would determine whether the fragile threads holding the town together would unravel completely or if a new, more terrifying tapestry would be woven in the darkness that had been unleashed.

Chapter 20: Embrace of Shadows

Ravenshade, plunged into chaos by the unforeseen malevolence, trembled on the brink of a nightmarish abyss. Isabella, Victor, and Detective Martin Harris stood as unwitting architects of the supernatural forces that now clawed at the very fabric of their reality. The air, once filled with whispers of redemption, now echoed with the wails of terror and the palpable darkness that seeped into every corner.

As the malevolent figure emerged from the shadows, the town square became a theater of horror. The once-tranquil streets transformed into a maze of fear, with panicked townspeople fleeing from the twisted manifestation of supernatural malevolence. The trio, their faces etched with horror, braced themselves for the onslaught of forces they had inadvertently unleashed.

The mansion, a looming silhouette against the night sky, seemed to watch the chaos unfold with an eerie stillness. The walls, once witnesses to centuries of secrets, now bore witness to the repercussions of tampering with forces beyond mortal comprehension. Isabella, Victor, and Detective Harris found themselves ensnared in a struggle that transcended the boundaries of the known.

The malevolent figure, a grotesque embodiment of ancient shadows, slithered through the square, leaving a trail of dread in its wake. Its contorted features spoke of a darkness that defied the laws of nature, and the very air seemed to ripple with an unsettling energy. Ravenshade, now a battleground between the forces of light and darkness, quivered under the weight of an impending nightmare.

Isabella, her heart pounding with a mixture of guilt and determination, locked eyes with Victor. The love that had once been a beacon of hope now faced a trial by fire. Detective Harris, the stalwart figure caught between the mundane and the supernatural, drew his weapon with a newfound urgency, ready to confront the malevolence that threatened to consume the town.

The townspeople, caught in the throes of panic, sought refuge wherever they could find it. The streets, once bustling with the everyday rhythm of life, now reverberated with the frenzied footsteps of those desperate to escape the encroaching darkness. Windows shuttered, doors slammed shut, and the once-cordial neighbors became strangers bound by a shared terror.

The trio, guided by instinct, led the charge against the malevolent force. The mansion's shadowy facade loomed ahead, a symbolic threshold between the known and the unknown. Isabella, her voice trembling yet resolute, urged the townspeople to rally together in the face of the supernatural onslaught.

As the malevolent figure closed in, the mansion's ancient secrets seemed to pulse with a malevolent glee. The walls, etched with the echoes of centuries, bore witness to the unraveling of a delicate balance. Isabella, Victor, and Detective Harris faced a choice—stand united against the shadows or succumb to the abyss that threatened to swallow Ravenshade whole.

The malevolent figure, sensing the resistance, unleashed a barrage of supernatural horrors. Shadows twisted and contorted, taking on monstrous forms that danced with an unnatural malevolence. The town's fate hung in the balance, teetering between salvation and damnation.

In the heart of Ravenshade, where the air crackled with an intensity that mirrored the collective fear, the trio confronted the malevolent force. The mansion, once a symbol of redemption, now stood as a battleground where the choices made would determine whether the town could emerge from the embrace of shadows or be forever consumed by the darkness that had been unleashed.

The malevolent force surged forward, its shadowy tendrils reaching out like insidious fingers, seeking to ensnare the hearts and minds of those it touched. The town square became a chaotic battleground, with the trio at the forefront, desperately trying to push back the encroaching darkness.

Isabella, her voice cutting through the dissonance, urged the townspeople to stand together against the malevolence. A fragile alliance formed amidst the chaos, with fear-stricken faces looking to the trio for guidance. The mansion, its ancient walls now a silent witness to the unfolding nightmare, seemed to exude a spectral energy that heightened the stakes of the cosmic struggle.

Detective Harris, his resolve hardened by the urgency of the situation, coordinated efforts to fortify the town square. Makeshift barricades were erected, and the echoes of gunfire reverberated through the night as the townspeople, armed with whatever they could find, prepared to face the malevolent force.

Victor, once burdened by his vampiric curse, now stood as a stalwart defender alongside Isabella. The love that had once been a source of redemption now became a beacon of resistance against the encroaching shadows. As the malevolent force bore down on them, the trio faced the realization that the consequences of their actions had ignited a supernatural war within the heart of Ravenshade.

The malevolent figure, now an amorphous mass of darkness, oozed through the barricades, evading conventional understanding. It whispered ancient incantations, unsettling the resolve of those who stood against it. The air, thick with a malevolent energy, seemed to pulse with the heartbeat of an otherworldly power.

The mansion, once a refuge of arcane knowledge, now revealed its true nature. Its corridors, twisted by the malevolence, became a labyrinth of shifting shadows and unforeseen horrors. Isabella, guided by an instinct that seemed to transcend mortal understanding, led the charge into the mansion, hoping to find a way to quell the supernatural onslaught.

As they delved into the mansion's depths, they encountered spectral manifestations and illusions that twisted the fabric of reality. Each step seemed to take them further into a nightmarish realm, where time and space became fluid, and the boundaries between the living and the supernatural blurred.

Detective Harris, his skepticism now replaced by a grim determination, faced the malevolent force head-on. The town's fate hung in the balance, and with every passing moment, the struggle intensified. The air, once thick with the stench of fear, now resonated with the battle cries of those who dared to challenge the abyss.

Isabella, Victor, and Detective Harris, their journey through the mansion fraught with terror and uncertainty, stumbled upon an ancient chamber at the heart of the building. A ghastly altar, adorned with arcane symbols, pulsed with an ominous energy. It became apparent that the mansion itself harbored the malevolent force, and severing its connection to the supernatural realm became the key to saving Ravenshade.

As the trio prepared to confront the malevolence at its source, the town square outside echoed with the desperate struggle of the townspeople. The battle against the shadows had become a test of resilience, where the choices made within the mansion would determine whether Ravenshade could emerge from the embrace of darkness or succumb to an eternal night.

In the ancient chamber at the heart of the mansion, Isabella, Victor, and Detective Harris confronted the malevolence that had taken residence

within its walls. The air felt heavy with the weight of unseen forces, and the trio braced themselves for a confrontation that would shape the town's destiny.

The altar, a macabre centerpiece of the supernatural energies that had tainted the mansion, pulsed with an otherworldly glow. Symbols etched into the stone seemed to writhe, and the very air shimmered with an unnatural energy. Isabella, drawing upon the knowledge gained from the ancient tomes, recognized that severing the connection between the mansion and the malevolent force was their only hope.

As they approached the altar, the malevolence manifested itself in a ghastly form—a shadowy apparition that seemed to draw from the darkest recesses of the human psyche. It whispered ancient curses, amplifying the fears and doubts of those who stood before it. Isabella, fortified by the love she shared with Victor, resisted the insidious whispers, determined to break the hold of the supernatural malevolence.

Victor, once tormented by his vampiric nature, found newfound strength in the face of the malevolence. The love he felt for Isabella became a shield against the shadows, and he stood alongside her, ready to confront the darkness that threatened to consume Ravenshade.

Detective Harris, a beacon of mortal resilience in the supernatural storm, gripped his weapon tightly. The detective, now fully aware of the extraordinary forces at play, faced the malevolence with a steadfast resolve. The town's fate rested on their shoulders, and the ancient chamber became the battlefield where mortal and supernatural clashed.

Isabella, her voice resonating with ancient incantations, began a ritual to sever the mansion's connection to the malevolent force. The air crackled with energy as the symbols on the altar reacted to the arcane power coursing through the room. Shadows recoiled, and the malevolent apparition writhed in agony, its form flickering like a dying flame.

The battle outside the mansion raged on. In the town square, the townspeople, armed with a newfound determination, faced the shadowy manifestations that sought to engulf Ravenshade. The air echoed with the sounds of struggle, the clash of improvised weapons, and the desperate cries of those fighting for their homes and loved ones.

As Isabella's ritual intensified, the mansion itself seemed to rebel against the malevolence. The walls groaned, and ethereal whispers filled the air. Detective Harris, sensing the pivotal moment, urged the townspeople to stand firm, reinforcing the barricades against the malevolent forces that threatened to spill out of the mansion.

Suddenly, a blinding light erupted from the altar, illuminating the chamber with an intensity that banished the shadows. Isabella, Victor, and Detective Harris felt the surge of power as the ritual reached its climax. The malevolent force, writhing in its death throes, let out a deafening scream that reverberated through the mansion.

In the town square, the townspeople witnessed the sudden stillness of the shadows. The malevolent apparitions dissipated, leaving behind an eerie calm. Ravenshade, once consumed by chaos, seemed to exhale as the supernatural threat lifted.

As the light from the altar subsided, Isabella, Victor, and Detective Harris emerged from the ancient chamber. The mansion, once a nexus of darkness, now stood silent, its secrets laid bare. The trio, weary yet triumphant, stepped into the town square, where the townspeople greeted them with a mixture of awe and gratitude.

Ravenshade, though scarred by the supernatural ordeal, stood on the threshold of a new beginning. Isabella, Victor, and Detective Harris, their journey through love, horror, and redemption now etched into the town's history, faced a community that had witnessed the extraordinary. The choices made within the mansion had sealed the town's fate, and as Ravenshade began to rebuild, the echoes of the supernatural struggle would linger as a cautionary tale—a reminder of the delicate balance between light and darkness.

A Vampire's Love

A Murder Mystery

By

Doug Hensley

Table Of Contents

Chapter 14: Love Conquers All
Chapter 15: The Final Clue
Chapter 16: The Chase
Chapter 18: The Tur
Chapter 19: The Confrontation
Chapter 20: Redemption

Chapter 1 A Stranger In Town

Ravenshade was draped in an ominous stillness as Victor's car rumbled along the desolate road, tires whispering against the gravel. The mansion, perched on the edge of town like a silent sentinel, cast long shadows that seemed to reach out, beckoning him into its enigmatic embrace.

Victor, a stranger with an air of mystery cloaked around him, felt a shiver run down his spine as he approached the grand entrance. The mansion loomed overhead, its towering façade bearing witness to untold secrets etched into the very stone. The air was heavy with a sense of foreboding, and the distant hooting of an owl added an eerie soundtrack to the unfolding narrative.

Entering the mansion felt like crossing a threshold into another realm. The creaking door echoed through the empty halls as Victor explored the dimly lit interior, shadows dancing along the walls like specters playing a macabre game. The air within seemed to carry whispers of forgotten tales, and a peculiar chill accompanied him, raising the hairs on the back of his neck.

In the heart of the mansion, Victor discovered a vast hall that seemed frozen in time. Dusty portraits adorned the walls, their subjects staring down with eyes that held untold stories. The grandeur of the past clashed with the decaying reality of the present, creating an unsettling atmosphere that sent shivers down Victor's spine.

As he ventured deeper, the mansion revealed its secrets. A cryptic library, filled with ancient volumes, beckoned him. The smell of aged leather and crumbling parchment hung in the air.

Victor's fingers traced over the spines of forgotten lore, each book a gateway to realms of knowledge long hidden.

The clock, a relic from a bygone era, ticked away in the background, its sound echoing through the empty corridors. Victor's footsteps reverberated with a haunting resonance as he explored the mansion's labyrinthine passages. The very architecture seemed to conspire against him, leading him into a maze of uncertainty.

In a secluded chamber, Victor stumbled upon an ancient coffin, its lid adorned with faded engravings. The air grew thicker as he approached, and a lingering scent of decay hinted at the passage of centuries. The coffin's presence became a visceral reminder of the mansion's dark history, a history that seemed to seep through the cracks in the walls.

As the night deepened, Victor's senses heightened. Muffled sounds, indistinct whispers, and faint echoes became the symphony of the supernatural. The mansion, a living entity with a pulse of its own, seemed to respond to Victor's presence, its secrets bubbling to the surface like a macabre revelation.

In the dim glow of a candle-lit chamber, Victor encountered a room adorned with ornate mirrors. Each reflection seemed to hold a glimpse into a distorted reality. Shadows flickered, and for a moment, Victor questioned whether the figure staring back at him was truly his own. The mirrors became portals to a world where reality and nightmare intertwined.

As the night wore on, an unsettling feeling settled over Victor. The mansion's ancient spirits seemed to stir, their ethereal presence palpable in the very air he breathed. The line between the living and the supernatural blurred, and Victor found himself caught in a web of spectral threads that seemed to tighten with every step.

In the heart of Ravenshade's foreboding mansion, Victor's journey into the unknown had just begun. The night held secrets that clung to the shadows, and the mansion, with its haunted corridors and ghostly whispers, became a stage for a supernatural drama that transcended the boundaries of the mortal realm. Little did Victor

that the events set in motion within the mansion's walls would weave a tale of love, horror, and redemption, where the very essence of his being would be entwined with the ancient forces that lurked in the darkness.

Chapter 2: The Funeral Director

The following day in Ravenshade dawned with an eerie stillness, as if the night had left behind a lingering specter that clung to the air. Victor, having explored the mansion's labyrinthine passages the previous night, found himself drawn to the peculiar atmosphere that enshrouded the town.

As he stepped outside, the town seemed to hold its breath. The morning mist curled around the cobblestone streets, creating an ethereal tapestry that obscured the edges of reality. The townspeople, their faces etched with a mixture of curiosity and suspicion, regarded Victor with wary glances as he made his way to the local funeral home.

The funeral home, a quaint establishment on the outskirts of town, exuded an aura of somberness that transcended the ordinary. Victor, now the proprietor, felt a sense of unease settle over him as he entered. The scent of aged wood and funeral lilies lingered in the air, and the creaking floorboards seemed to echo with the weight of countless mournful footsteps.

Victor's arrival didn't go unnoticed. The townspeople, gossiping in hushed tones, watched as he assumed his role within the funeral home. The atmosphere within the establishment grew tense, as if the very walls were privy to the ancient secrets that had unfolded within the mansion the night before.

The funeral home became a stage for a macabre drama. Victor, surrounded by the trappings of death, delved into the somber duties that awaited him. The coffins, each one a vessel for the departed, held a silent testimony to the passage of time and the inevitable march toward the unknown.

As the day unfolded, a peculiar pattern emerged. Each funeral seemed to carry an undertone of mystery, a whisper of unnatural finality that sent shivers down Victor's spine. The townspeople, mourning their loved ones, regarded him with a suspicion that mirrored the town's collective unease.

Detective Martin Harris, the town's astute investigator, couldn't ignore the strange occurrences that now seemed to center around Victor. The deaths, while individually unremarkable, formed a disturbing pattern that raised the detective's suspicions. The eerie coincidence of death and Victor's presence cast a shadow over Ravenshade, and Detective Harris couldn't shake the feeling that the stranger in their midst held a key to the unexplained.

As Victor navigated the delicate rituals of death, Isabella, a local woman of captivating beauty, entered the funeral home seeking solace for her recently departed grandmother. Victor, drawn to Isabella's ethereal presence, felt a connection that transcended the boundaries of the ordinary. Isabella, in turn, sensed something otherworldly about Victor, a magnetic pull that defied rational explanation.

Their encounter became a poignant moment amidst the funereal gloom. Isabella's tearful eyes held a mixture of grief and curiosity, and Victor, unable to shake the weight of the supernatural that clung to him, found himself drawn to her vulnerability. Little did they know, their fates had become intertwined in a cosmic dance that echoed the mysteries of the night.

As the day waned, Victor and Isabella's connection deepened. The funeral home, now a nexus of the town's secrets, became a stage for a drama that unfolded beneath the surface. Unbeknownst to them, Detective Harris, fueled by his growing suspicions, began to investigate the mysterious deaths that seemed to trail in Victor's wake.

Night descended upon Ravenshade like a shroud, and the funeral home, now cloaked in darkness, became a focal point for the supernatural forces that seemed to awaken with the setting sun. Victor, haunted by the events of the night before, found himself entangled in a web of love, death, and the unexplained, where the boundaries between the living and the dead blurred into a tapestry of terror that hinted at the ancient forces lurking within the town's very sou

Chapter 3: Love at First Sight

The moon hung high in the night sky as Victor closed the creaking door of the funeral home, its echo resonating through the dimly lit halls. The town of Ravenshade slept, unaware of the supernatural undercurrents that pulsed through its veins. Victor, burdened by the weight of the funeral home's ominous atmosphere, felt a growing sense of unease as he traversed the silent streets.

As he walked, shadows danced across the cobblestone pathways, casting an otherworldly glow on the facades of the buildings. The mansion, looming on the outskirts like a dark sentinel, seemed to watch over the town with a silent malevolence. Victor's footsteps echoed through the quiet, unsettling the night's delicate equilibrium.

Isabella's haunting beauty lingered in Victor's thoughts, and the enigmatic connection they shared played on his mind like a haunting melody. The night air, thick with a spectral energy, whispered secrets that seemed to tangle with the threads of his consciousness. He questioned the nature of his own existence, a disquieting realization settling within him.

As Victor approached the mansion, an unnatural chill clung to the air. The grand entrance, now shrouded in darkness, beckoned him with a foreboding allure. The mansion's ancient walls seemed to pulse with an energy that transcended the mortal realm. Each step he took echoed through the halls like a heartbeat, resonating with an unseen force that slumbered within.

Entering the mansion felt like stepping into a realm untouched by time. The air within was heavy with the scent of aged wood and the faint traces of ancient secrets. Victor's footsteps reverberated through the grand corridors, and the mansion seemed to awaken with a subtle malevolence that clung to the very air he breathed.

In the heart of the mansion, Victor found himself drawn to a forgotten chamber. The room, hidden behind layers of dust and decay, exuded an otherworldly aura. An old mirror, its glass tarnished with age, reflected a distorted version of Victor's own reflection. The figure staring back seemed to ripple with a supernatural resonance.

As Victor delved deeper into the mansion's mysteries, the shadows seemed to come alive. Whispers echoed through the corridors, carrying ancient incantations that reverberated with an unsettling power. The very walls of the mansion seemed to breathe, exhaling the secrets of centuries long past.

The mansion's archives revealed cryptic manuscripts and arcane symbols that hinted at a supernatural legacy intertwined with Ravenshade's history. Victor, driven by an insatiable curiosity, translated the forgotten texts, each word revealing a fragment of a cosmic tapestry that threatened to unravel the town's reality.

The night wore on, and as the clock in the mansion's grand hall ticked away, Victor's exploration led him to a hidden chamber beneath the mansion. The air in the chamber was thick with a palpable malevolence, and the ground seemed to vibrate with an ancient power that clawed its way to the surface.

Within the chamber, Victor discovered an ancient artifact—an ornate chalice adorned with symbols that mirrored those in the mansion's archives. The artifact seemed to radiate a supernatural energy, and its presence hinted at a ritualistic purpose that sent shivers down Victor's spine.

Unbeknownst to him, Detective Harris, fueled by an insatiable curiosity of his own, delved into the town's history. The detective's investigation unearthed tales of a vampire curse that had haunted Ravenshade for centuries, a curse that seemed to align with the mysterious events surrounding Victor and the ancient artifact.

As Victor studied the artifact, a sudden chill enveloped the chamber. The shadows seemed to coalesce into grotesque shapes that slithered across the stone floor. Unearthly whispers echoed through the darkness, and the malevolence that had slept within the mansion stirred with an insidious intent.

The artifact, a key to the supernatural forces that lurked beneath Ravenshade, became a conduit for a spectral energy that surged through the chamber. The air crackled with an ominous electricity, and the chalice seemed to resonate with the very heartbeat of the town. Victor, caught in the grip of the supernatural maelstrom, felt the boundary between the living and the dead blur into a nightmarish amalgamation.

As the clock struck midnight, a ritual long dormant was set in motion. The mansion's ancient secrets, entwined with Victor's own existence, unleashed a terror that seeped into the very fabric of Ravenshade. The town, now a stage for a supernatural symphony, trembled on the brink of an unspeakable abyss as the forces that had slept for centuries awoke with a malevolent hunger.

Chapter 4: Forbidden Desires

The night unfolded in Ravenshade, a canvas of darkness painted with an otherworldly brush. Victor, caught in the grip of the supernatural forces that had awakened within the mansion, felt a sense of dread as the town slumbered, oblivious to the malevolence that now pulsed beneath its cobblestone streets.

In the mansion's hidden chamber, the ancient artifact's resonance intensified. The chalice, cradled in Victor's hands, seemed to throb with an unholy heartbeat. Shadows writhed on the chamber walls, taking on grotesque forms that whispered of forgotten rituals and an unspeakable power that transcended the mortal realm.

As the spectral energy surged, Victor's senses heightened. Unseen whispers echoed through the chamber, a chorus of disembodied voices that seemed to taunt his very existence. The air grew thick with a supernatural tension, and the artifacts within the chamber seemed to come alive with a malevolent energy.

Detective Harris, unaware of the supernatural forces at play, delved deeper into his investigation. The town's history unraveled before him, revealing a dark tapestry of curses and rituals that hinted at a cycle of terror bound to the mansion. The detective's determination clashed with the ominous events unfolding in the hidden corners of Ravenshade.

In the heart of the town, Isabella, restless in her slumber, found herself haunted by vivid dreams. Nightmares of shadowy figures and ethereal whispers tormented her sleep. Unbeknownst to her, the connection she shared with Victor acted as a conduit for the supernatural energies that now threatened to consume Ravenshade.

As the clock struck the witching hour, the mansion's ancient walls seemed to groan with an unholy resonance. Victor, compelled by an unseen force, began a ritual with the artifact. Symbols etched in the chamber's stone floor illuminated with an otherworldly glow. The chalice, now a vessel for dark energies, cast eerie shadows that danced with a demonic glee.

Outside, the town was cloaked in an unnatural stillness. The moon cast an eerie pallor on the streets as spectral entities emerged from the shadows. Unseen by the slumbering townspeople, these ethereal beings drifted through the night, drawn to the mansion like moths to a malevolent flame.

Victor, his eyes reflecting the flickering candlelight, chanted incantations that resonated with the ancient forces. The chamber became a portal to a realm beyond, where the line between the living and the dead blurred into a nightmarish symphony. The town, caught in the grip of a supernatural tempest, teetered on the precipice of a cataclysmic event.

Isabella, her sleep disturbed by the escalating malevolence, found herself drawn to the mansion. Guided by an unseen force, she moved through the silent streets like a sleepwalker. Her connection with Victor became a conduit for the supernatural energies, and as she approached the mansion, a chorus of disembodied voices echoed in her mind.

Detective Harris, sensing a disturbance, rushed toward the mansion. Unbeknownst to him, the spectral entities that now roamed Ravenshade cast a malevolent gaze upon his determined figure. The detective, fueled by a sense of duty, ventured into the heart of the supernatural storm, oblivious to the terror that awaited.

Within the mansion's hidden chamber, the ritual reached its crescendo. The artifact's malevolent energy surged through Victor, intertwining with his very essence. The air crackled with an otherworldly electricity as the boundaries between the living and the dead dissolved.

Isabella, now within the mansion's ominous embrace, felt the spectral forces converge upon her. Shadows clung to her like ethereal tendrils, and the disembodied voices whispered cryptic prophecies that echoed in the caverns of her mind. Unseen hands seemed to guide her, and the mansion's ancient walls bore witness to a cosmic dance between mortals and the supernatural.

Detective Harris, arriving at the mansion's grand entrance, sensed an unnatural chill that defied reason. The spectral entities, drawn to his presence, coalesced into an ephemeral phalanx that blocked his path. Undeterred, the detective pressed on, unaware that he stood on the threshold of a realm beyond his comprehension.

As the ritual unfolded, the mansion became a focal point for the convergence of ancient energies. The town's fate hung in the balance, and the malevolence that had slumbered within the mansion for centuries now threatened to spill into every corner of Ravenshade. The night, once quiet and foreboding, erupted into a supernatural symphony that reverberated through the very soul of the town.

Chapter 5: A Series of Murders

In the heart of Ravenshade, the night held its breath as the supernatural forces unleashed by the ritual within the mansion continued to weave a dark tapestry over the town. The moon cast an eerie glow on the cobblestone streets, and a chilling wind whispered through the silent alleys, carrying with it an otherworldly resonance.

. The artifact, now pulsating with malevolent energy, seemed to amplify the spectral forces that danced through the air. The shadows within the mansion writhed with an insidious intent, merging with the ancient spirits that had slumbered for centuries.

Isabella, guided by an unseen force, approached the mansion's entrance. The air crackled with an ethereal energy, and the very fabric of reality seemed to ripple as she crossed the threshold. The disembodied voices echoed in her mind, weaving a haunting chorus that spoke of prophecies and the convergence of mortal and supernatural destinies.

Detective Harris, undeterred by the spectral entities that blocked his path, pressed forward. The spectral beings, drawn to the detective's resilience, flickered like phantoms in the moonlit night. The mansion, now a nexus of dark energies, seemed to breathe with a life of its own, anticipating the climax of the ritual that unfolded within its walls.

As the town slept, oblivious to the malevolence that loomed, the mansion's arcane energies intensified. The ritual, a cosmic dance between Victor, Isabella, and the ancient forces, reached a fever pitch. Symbols on the chamber's stone floor pulsed with an unholy light, casting grotesque shadows that danced in rhythm with the supernatural symphony.

Victor, caught in the grip of the ritual's crescendo, felt the very fabric of his existence unravel. The artifact, now fused with his essence, became a conduit for an unimaginable power. His mind resonated with the ancient spirits, and the mansion's walls seemed to close in as if bearing witness to a celestial reckoning.

Isabella, within the mansion's embrace, became a vessel for the supernatural forces. Her senses heightened, and the dis-embodied voices guided her through the labyrinthine corridors. Shadows clung to her like a spectral cloak, and the air around her seemed to shimmer with an otherworldly luminescence.

Detective Harris, now standing at the mansion's threshold, sensed the malevolence that permeated the air. The spectral entities, drawn to his presence, formed an ethereal barrier that challenged the detective's very sanity. Undeterred, Harris pressed forward, determined to unravel the mysteries that lurked within the heart of Ravenshade.

The town itself seemed to respond to the ritual's intensity. Unseen forces permeated the air, and the very buildings seemed to exhale the collective fear that now hung over Ravenshade like a suffocating mist. The supernatural storm that brewed within the mansion's walls threatened to engulf the town in a cosmic tempest.

Within the hidden chamber, the ritual's climax approached. The artifact, now a conduit for the ancient forces, emitted a blinding light that spilled into the corridors. Victor, his body now marked by ethereal patterns, chanted incantations that echoed through the very fabric of reality. The air crackled with an energy that transcended the laws of nature.

Isabella, guided to the ritual's epicenter, felt a surge of power within her. The spectral cloak that clung to her seemed to meld with the shadows, creating an otherworldly silhouette that moved in tandem with the ritual's rhythm. The disembodied voices reached a crescendo, their whispers now a cacophony that reverberated through her very soul.

Detective Harris, crossing the threshold into the mansion, witnessed the supernatural spectacle that unfolded before him. The spectral entities, now drawn to the detective like moths to a flame, seemed to shift and waver as if uncertain of their purpose. The very air seemed to ripple with an unseen force, challenging Harris's perceptions of reality.

As the ritual reached its apex, a rift in the fabric of reality opened within the mansion's chamber. Victor, Isabella, and Detective Harris stood at the precipice of a cosmic abyss. The artifact's blinding light merged with the shadows, creating a swirling vortex that seemed to devour the very essence of the town.

Ravenshade, now caught in the grip of a supernatural cataclysm, trembled on the brink of an unfathomable transformation. The town's destiny hung in the balance as the ritual, an ancient dance between mortal and supernatural forces, threatened to rewrite the very laws of existence. The night, once a canvas of foreboding darkness, now crackled with an otherworldly energy that signaled the dawn of a malevolent era.

Chapter 6: The Detective's Hunch

Within the mansion's hidden chamber, the swirling vortex created by the ritual's climax enveloped Victor, Isabella, and Detective Harris. The light and ethereal shadows merged, creating a cosmic maelstrom that seemed to defy the laws of reality. The very fabric of Ravenshade trembled as the supernatural forces surged through the town.

As Victor, now marked by the arcane patterns etched into his skin, stood at the epicenter of the vortex, he felt an overwhelming surge of power. The disembodied voices echoed in his mind, their whispers a symphony of ancient secrets and forgotten prophecies. The mansion's walls seemed to breathe with a malevolent energy that mirrored the pulse of his own supernatural essence.

Isabella, caught in the cosmic tempest, felt the spectral forces intertwining with her very being. The shadows that clung to her took on a life of their own, weaving a surreal dance that mirrored the chaos within the hidden chamber. The disembodied voices now resonated with a haunting clarity, guiding her through the shifting dimensions of the supernatural vortex.

Detective Harris, his senses overwhelmed by the otherworldly spectacle, struggled to maintain his grip on reality. The spectral entities that had blocked his path now circled him like ethereal vultures, their forms flickering with an unsettling uncertainty. The detective, fueled by an unyielding determination, pressed on through the swirling chaos.

Outside the mansion, the town responded to the supernatural upheaval. The night sky above Ravenshade churned with ominous clouds, and an otherworldly wind whispered through the silent streets. The townspeople, oblivious to the cosmic drama unfolding within the mansion, slept on, their dreams haunted by nightmarish visions.

Within the vortex, time seemed to lose its meaning. The boundaries between past, present, and future blurred, creating a surreal dreamscape. Victor, Isabella, and Detective Harris found themselves navigating a spectral landscape where reality itself seemed to shift like sand beneath their feet.

As the trio moved through the cosmic tempest, they glimpsed fragments of Ravenshade's history. Scenes from centuries past unfolded before their eyes – the town's founding, ancient rituals, and the struggles of those who had faced the supernatural forces that lurked within the mansion. The disembodied voices whispered tales of love, betrayal, and the unbreakable bond between the town and the darkness that clung to it.

Isabella, guided by the spectral voices, witnessed her own lineage intertwined with the town's ancient mysteries. Faces of ancestors long forgotten appeared in ethereal visions, each one marked by the same haunting beauty that she possessed. The supernatural forces that coursed through her veins seemed to echo through generations, a legacy she had unknowingly inherited.

Detective Harris, a mortal caught in the cosmic currents, saw glimpses of his own investigations into the supernatural. The unsolved mysteries of Ravenshade, the eerie occurrences that had eluded rational explanation, now seemed to form a tapestry of malevolence that stretched across time. The detective's pursuit of truth had unwittingly led him to the precipice of an abyss beyond his understanding.

Victor, marked by both the vampiric curse and the new-found supernatural power, felt the weight of centuries pressing upon him. Visions of his own origin, the night he was turned into a vampire, and the struggles that had defined his immortal existence flickered like ghostly apparitions. The ritual, it seemed, had become a conduit for the convergence of his own tormented history.

As the trio navigated the shifting dimensions, they encountered spectral entities that seemed to embody the very essence of Ravenshade's darkness. Ghostly figures, each one a reflection of the town's haunted legacy, reached out with ethereal hands that sought to pull them deeper into the cosmic vortex. The disembodied voices urged them forward, promising revelations and a reckoning with the ancient forces that held Ravenshade in their thrall.

The visions within the vortex grew increasingly surreal. Isabella, Victor, and Detective Harris found themselves in surreal landscapes where reality twisted and turned like a kaleidoscope of nightmares. Faces of long-dead townspeople whispered secrets, and shadows danced in macabre celebrations of ancient rituals.

The town's history unfolded in a non-linear narrative, revealing the cyclical nature of the supernatural forces that plagued Ravenshade. Each generation, it seemed, faced its own version of the cosmic tempest, and the trio now stood at the nexus of a convergence that threatened to rewrite the very fabric of their existence.

As the visions intensified, the trio approached a spectral gateway that shimmered with an otherworldly light. The disembodied voices, now a chorus of echoes from across time, guided them toward the gateway, promising answers to the mysteries that had haunted Ravenshade for centuries.

Crossing the threshold, Isabella, Victor, and Detective Harris found themselves in a surreal realm that defied all logic. The cosmic tempest, now a distant echo, left them standing in an otherworldly landscape where the very laws of nature seemed to be dictated by the whims of supernatural forces.

The gateway, it appeared, led to the heart of the ancient energies that bound Ravenshade to its haunted legacy. Before them stood an ethereal representation of the town, a mirrored version that pulsed with a malevolent energy. The disembodied voices, now a unified chorus, revealed the purpose of the ritual – to confront the ancient forces and decide the fate of Ravenshade once and for all.

The trio, now standing at the crossroads of mortal and supernatural destinies, faced a surreal entity that embodied the darkness that had clung to the town for centuries. The entity, a shape-shifting manifestation of malevolence, seemed to draw upon the collective fears and nightmares of Ravenshade's history.

The disembodied voices urged Victor, Isabella, and Detective Harris to confront the entity, to unravel the cosmic threads that bound them to the town's destiny. The entity, aware of their presence, morphed into grotesque forms that reflected the deepest fears and regrets of each individual.

Isabella, guided by an inner strength

Chapter 7: Love Blossoms

In the surreal realm where reality danced with the whims of supernatural forces, Isabella, Victor, and Detective Harris stood before the shape-shifting entity that embodied Ravenshade's haunting legacy. The ethereal representation of the town pulsed with a malevolent energy, and the disembodied voices, now a unified chorus, urged them to confront the ancient forces that held the town in their thrall.

Isabella, her inner strength fortified by the spectral voices that guided her, faced the shape-shifting entity with unwavering determination. The entity, aware of her connection to the supernatural energies, morphed into unsettling forms that mirrored Isabella's deepest fears and insecurities.

Images of her ancestors, their haunting beauty twisted into grotesque visages, materialized around her. Shadows clung to their spectral forms, whispering of ancient curses and the price paid for the beauty that had become a legacy. Isabella, undeterred, saw through the illusions, recognizing the entity's attempts to manipulate her with echoes of the past.

As Isabella confronted the entity, she delved into her own memories, unraveling the emotional tapestry that wove her connection to Ravenshade. The disembodied voices, a supportive chorus in her mind, guided her through the labyrinth of her own fears. Faces of loved ones, the echoes of laughter and sorrow, formed a mosaic that challenged the malevolence before her.

The shape-shifting entity, sensing Isabella's resilience, intensified its efforts. The surreal landscape transformed, distorting into nightmarish scenes that mirrored the darkest corners of Raven-shade's history. Isabella navigated through illusions of betrayal, loss, and the haunting beauty that had defined her lineage.

Unbeknownst to her, Victor and Detective Harris faced their own trials in the cosmic realm. Victor, still marked by the vampiric curse and the newfound supernatural power, confronted illusions of his own victims. Faces of those he had fed upon through-out the centuries materialized, their accusing gazes reflecting the weight of his immortal existence.

Detective Harris, a mortal in a realm beyond his understanding, faced illusions of unsolved cases that haunted his investigative career. The spectral entities that circled him took on the forms of victims and perpetrators alike, their phantasmal accusations echoing through the surreal landscape.

The disembodied voices, a guiding presence in their minds, urged Victor and Detective Harris to confront the illusions and unravel the cosmic threads that bound them to Ravenshade's destiny. Each trial presented a test of their resolve, forcing them to face the consequences of their actions and the shadows that lurked within their own psyches.

As Isabella, Victor, and Detective Harris navigated through the illusions, the cosmic realm seemed to shift in response to their inner struggles. The surreal landscape twisted and turned, creat-ing a disorienting maze of fears and revelations. The very fabric of the town's haunting legacy seemed to pulse with a malevolent energy that sought to ensnare them.

Isabella, drawing strength from the voices within her mind, confronted the shape-shifting entity in its final form. The illusions shattered, revealing the entity's true nature – a manifestation of the collective fears and regrets that had woven Ravenshade's destiny. The entity, stripped of its illusions, writhed in a spectral dance that mirrored the town's tumultuous history.

Victor and Detective Harris, having conquered their own trials, joined Isabella in facing the entity. The disembodied voices, now a triumphant chorus, urged them to channel the supernatural energies within and confront the ancient forces that had plagued Ravenshade for centuries.

As the trio focused their resolve, a surge of power emanated from the cosmic realm. The town's haunting legacy seemed to recoil, and the surreal landscape fractured like a shattered mirror. Ravenshade, now suspended in a moment between reality and the supernatural, awaited the trio's decision – a decision that would determine the town's ultimate fate.

The disembodied voices, their whispers now a gentle melody, guided Isabella, Victor, and Detective Harris toward a spectral gateway. The gateway shimmered with an ethereal light, offering a path back to Ravenshade's tangible reality. The trio, now intertwined with the town's destiny, hesitated before taking the final step.

Behind them, the shape-shifting entity convulsed in a spectral dance. The disembodied voices echoed a warning – the ancient forces, while subdued, still lingered. The town's fate hung in the balance, and the trio faced a choice that would resonate through the fabric of Ravenshade's existence.

Isabella, her connection to the supernatural energies now a profound understanding, made a decision that would shape the town's destiny. She reached out to the spectral gateway, channeling the power within her to bridge the cosmic realm with Ravenshade's reality. The disembodied voices, their whispers now a gentle breeze, conveyed a sense of acceptance and resolution.

The gateway pulsed with an otherworldly light as Isabella, Victor, and Detective Harris stepped through. The cosmic tempest, now subsided, left behind a town forever changed. The surreal landscape dissolved into the familiar streets of Ravenshade, but the echoes of the cosmic realm lingered in the air.

Ravenshade, now free from the malevolent energies that had plagued it for centuries, woke from its haunted slumber. The moon cast a soft glow on the cobblestone streets, and a gentle breeze carried with it the scent of a town reborn. The disembodied voices, now a distant murmur, faded into the background, leaving behind a sense of closure and renewal.

Isabella, Victor, and Detective Harris found themselves standing in the heart of Ravenshade, their connection to the supernatural energies now a shared legacy. The town, once bound by a cyclical curse, seemed to breathe with a newfound vitality. The spectral gateway, now closed, left behind a subtle resonance that hinted at the town's enduring connection to the cosmic forces.

As the trio reflected on their journey, they realized that Ravenshade's haunting legacy had been transformed. The town, no longer a prisoner of its past, now stood as a testament to the resilience of mortal and supernatural alike. The disembodied voices, their whispers now a gentle melody that harmonized with the town's heartbeat, conveyed a sense of gratitude and closure.

The night sky above Ravenshade shimmered with an ethereal glow, and the moon cast a luminous embrace over the town. Isabella, Victor, and Detective Harris, their shared journey etched into the fabric of Ravenshade's history, walked into the moonlit night with a sense of unity and purpose. The town, once ensnared by a supernatural curse, now stood as a beacon of hope in the face of the unknown.

Chapter 8: The Vampire's Dilemma

The night in Ravenshade bore witness to a profound transformation. Isabella, Victor, and Detective Harris, having confronted the cosmic forces that had haunted the town, found themselves standing in the moonlit streets, a shared sense of unity and purpose binding them together. Yet, the echoes of the cosmic realm lingered, and Ravenshade, now free from its malevolent past, braced for the unpredictable aftermath of their journey.

As the trio moved through the silent streets, the town seemed to exhale a collective sigh of relief. The moon cast long shadows that danced on the cobblestone pathways, and a gentle breeze carried with it the scent of renewal. The air itself felt charged with an otherworldly energy, a reminder that the supernatural currents still pulsed beneath Ravenshade's surface.

The mansion, once a focal point of ancient energies, loomed on the outskirts like a silent sentinel. Its grandeur, now stripped of the malevolence that had clung to it for centuries, stood as a testament to the town's newfound resilience. Isabella, Victor, and Detective Harris approached the mansion, drawn by an unspoken understanding that their journey was far from over.

Inside the mansion, the air felt different. The ancient walls, once imbued with a spectral malevolence, now exuded a solemn calmness. The hidden chamber, where the ritual had unfolded, stood as a testament to the cosmic forces that had intertwined with the town's destiny. The trio entered cautiously, the echoes of their footsteps resonating through the silent halls.

As they explored the mansion, subtle remnants of the supernatural lingered. Victor, still marked by the vampiric curse, felt a resonance with the ancient energies. Isabella, guided by her newfound connection to the cosmic forces, sensed an underlying current that pulsed beneath the mansion's surface. Detective Harris, a mortal caught in the crossfire of the supernatural, navigated through the shadows with a sense of wary curiosity.

In the grand hall, a peculiar artifact caught their attention. A centuries-old tapestry adorned the wall, depicting scenes from Ravenshade's haunted history. Isabella, Victor, and Detective Harris studied the tapestry, each thread unraveling the town's cyclical struggle with the supernatural. Faces of long-forgotten townspeople stared back, their expressions frozen in an eternal dance between fear and resilience.

The artifact, now a relic of Ravenshade's transformed destiny, seemed to resonate with the trio. Isabella, her connection to the cosmic forces attuned, touched the tapestry, and the fabric seemed to ripple with a subtle energy. Victor, compelled by an ancient familiarity, traced the patterns with his fingers, the images sparking distant memories of his immortal existence. Detective Harris, ever the rational investigator, observed the artifact with a sense of intrigue and caution.

As the trio delved deeper into the mansion's mysteries, an unsettling realization dawned upon them. The cosmic forces that had been confronted in the surreal realm were not entirely subdued. Instead, they lingered like dormant embers, waiting for an opportune moment to rekindle the supernatural currents within Ravenshade.

The disembodied voices, now a distant murmur, hinted at the delicate balance that the trio had achieved. Ravenshade's fate, they conveyed, was intricately tied to the choices made in the aftermath of the ritual. The mansion, once a conduit for ancient energies, now stood as a nexus where the town's past and future intersected.

Isabella, Victor, and Detective Harris faced a choice that would echo through the town's history. The artifact in the grand hall seemed to beckon them, its presence a silent reminder of the cosmic threads that bound Ravenshade to the supernatural. The disembodied voices, now a subtle whisper, urged them to decide the town's ultimate destiny.

As they deliberated, a sudden chill enveloped the mansion. Shadows danced on the walls, and the air seemed to thicken with a spectral energy. The cosmic currents, having lingered in the shadows, now stirred with an ominous intent. The mansion, once a haven for the supernatural, became a stage for the unfolding drama that would determine Ravenshade's fate.

Isabella, her connection to the cosmic forces resonating with the artifact, felt a surge of power within her. The disembodied voices, now a gentle breeze that rustled through the halls, conveyed a sense of guidance. Victor, marked by both the vampiric curse and the ancient energies, stood at a crossroads where his immortal existence intersected with the town's destiny. Detective Harris, a mortal caught in the cosmic currents, faced the uncertainty of navigating a realm beyond rational explanation.

The artifact in the grand hall seemed to pulse with an ethereal light, its patterns shifting like constellations in the night sky. Isabella, guided by the subtle energy that emanated from the tapestry, reached out. Her touch, a conduit for the cosmic forces, triggered a reaction that sent ripples through the mansion.

As Isabella touched the artifact, a spectral gateway opened within the grand hall. The disembodied voices, now a harmonious melody, conveyed a sense of inevitability. The town's destiny, it seemed, rested on the trio's willingness to embrace the supernatural currents and navigate Ravenshade's uncertain future.

Victor, drawn by an ancient familiarity, stepped through the spectral gateway. The mansion's walls seemed to dissolve around him, and he found himself standing in a surreal realm where reality intertwined with the cosmic forces. Isabella followed, her connection to the supernatural energies.

Chapter 9: The Investigation Heats Up

the surreal realm beyond the spectral gateway, Isabella and Victor found themselves immersed in a cosmic landscape where reality intertwined with the supernatural forces that had haunted Ravenshade. The disembodied voices, now a gentle chorus that echoed through the ethereal expanse, guided them toward the heart of the town's uncertain destiny.

As Isabella and Victor navigated through the cosmic landscape, the very fabric of reality seemed to shift and warp. The surroundings fluctuated between familiar scenes of Ravenshade and surreal manifestations of the town's haunting history. Shadows danced on the periphery, and distant whispers carried echoes of forgotten secrets.

The disembodied voices, their guidance a subtle current in the cosmic winds, revealed that the duo had entered the nexus where Ravenshade's past and future converged. The decisions made within this cosmic realm would shape the town's destiny, determining whether it remained bound to the supernatural or embraced a new existence free from the malevolent energies that had plagued it for centuries.

Meanwhile, back in the mansion, Detective Harris faced the challenge of crossing the spectral gateway. The air within the grand hall crackled with an otherworldly energy as he approached the artifact. A sense of trepidation accompanied him, for he was a mortal venturing into a realm that transcended the boundaries of his understanding.

As Detective Harris touched the artifact, the spectral gateway opened before him. The mansion's surroundings dissolved into a surreal expanse, and he stepped through, finding himself in the same cosmic landscape that Isabella and Victor now explored. The disembodied voices, recognizing his mortal presence, murmured words of caution and encouragement.

Together, the trio moved through the cosmic realm, guided by the ethereal currents that pulsed beneath Ravenshade's supernatural tapestry. The landscape became a mosaic of the town's memories and the trio's shared experiences. Visions of the ritual, the surreal trials within the vortex, and glimpses of the mansion's haunted history played out like a surreal play.

The disembodied voices, now a harmonious melody that resonated with the trio's journey, hinted at the choices awaiting them. They spoke of a cosmic balance that needed to be maintained, cautioning against the allure of unchecked power. Ravenshade, it seemed, had the potential for both redemption and descent into a darker unknown.

As the trio approached the nexus, the cosmic currents intensified. The surreal landscape took on an otherworldly brilliance, and a distant hum echoed through the expanse. Shadows gathered, coalescing into spectral entities that seemed to observe the trio's every move. The disembodied voices, their chorus now a crescendo of anticipation, urged the trio to confront the cosmic forces that lingered within Ravenshade's essence.

Isabella, Victor, and Detective Harris stood before an ethereal gateway that shimmered with an otherworldly glow. The disembodied voices conveyed that this gateway led to the very heart of Ravenshade's destiny. It was a threshold where the trio would face a choice that would resonate through the town's history, either sealing its fate with the supernatural or embracing a new beginning.

The cosmic forces, aware of the trio's presence, manifested in spectral forms that mirrored the town's darkest fears. Shadows twisted and contorted, taking on grotesque shapes that seemed to embody the malevolent energies that had plagued Ravenshade for centuries. The disembodied voices, now a resolute chant, urged the trio to stand firm against the encroaching darkness.

Isabella, her connection to the supernatural energies amplifying, felt the weight of Ravenshade's history upon her shoulders. Visions of the town's struggles and the spectral entities that had haunted its streets flashed before her eyes. The disembodied voices, now a guiding force in her mind, urged her to embrace the cosmic currents and make a choice that transcended mortal and supernatural boundaries.

Victor, marked by both the vampiric curse and the ancient energies, grappled with his immortal existence. Memories of his victims and the centuries of solitude intertwined with visions of redemption and a longing for a connection to humanity. The disembodied voices, recognizing his internal turmoil, whispered words of acceptance and transformation.

Detective Harris, a mortal facing the cosmic unknown, confronted the shadows of unsolved mysteries that had defined his investigative career. Spectral entities, embodying the enigmas that had eluded rational explanation, circled him like phantoms of the past. The disembodied voices, now a reassuring presence, conveyed that the answers he sought lay within the choices made in the cosmic nexus.

As the trio faced the spectral gateway, the cosmic forces intensified their presence. The surreal landscape quivered, and the ethereal glow of the gateway seemed to pulsate with a rhythmic energy. The disembodied voices, now a guiding symphony, echoed a final warning – the choice made within the cosmic nexus would bind Ravenshade's destiny to either redemption or an eternal struggle with the supernatural.

With resolve in their hearts, Isabella, Victor, and Detective Harris stepped through the spectral gateway. The cosmic currents enveloped them, and they found themselves standing in a surreal realm where the very essence of Ravenshade's destiny seemed to converge.

The disembodied voices, now a harmonious chorus that resonated with the trio's every step, guided them toward the cosmic nexus. The surroundings shifted between familiar scenes of the town and abstract manifestations of the supernatural forces that lurked within. The trio stood at the epicenter of Ravenshade's history, where past, present, and future coalesced in a cosmic dance.

Before them, an ancient entity materialized – a manifestation of the town's haunting legacy. The entity, a shape-shifting specter of malevolence, twisted and morphed in response to the trio's presence. The disembodied voices, now a unified force, conveyed that the entity embodied the collective fears and struggles of Ravenshade.

Isabella, Victor, and Detective Harris confronted the entity with a shared sense of purpose. The cosmic currents surged around them, creating a tempest of spectral energies. The disembodied voices, now a triumphant chant, urged the trio to channel the choices made in the cosmic nexus and face the entity with a determination that transcended mortal limitations.

As the trio confronted the entity, a surreal battle unfolded in the cosmic realm. Shadows clashed, and echoes of Ravenshade's history played out in spectral flashes. The disembodied voices, their chorus now an anthem of resilience, guided the trio in weaving a cosmic tapestry that sought to redefine the town's destiny.

Isabella, drawing upon her connection to the supernatural energies, reached into the very fabric of Ravenshade's essence. Her touch sent ripples through the cosmic currents, and the entity recoiled in response. The disembodied voices, now a harmonious melody that resonated with the trio's unity, conveyed that Isabella's choice had the power to redefine the town's relationship with the supernatural.

Victor, marked by both the vampiric curse and the ancient energies, confronted the entity with a newfound understanding. His immortal existence, once a source of isolation, became a conduit for transformation. The disembodied voices, recognizing Victor's journey of redemption, whispered words of acceptance and a promise of renewal.

Detective Harris, a mortal navigating the cosmic unknown, faced the shadows of unsolved mysteries with a determination that defied rational explanation. The spectral entities that circled him seemed to waver in the face of his unwavering resolve. The disembodied voices, now a supportive presence that echoed through

Chapter 10: Unraveling Secrets

The cosmic battle within the surreal realm reached its crescendo as Isabella, Victor, and Detective Harris confronted the shape-shifting entity embodying Ravenshade's haunting legacy. The spectral tempest surged around them, casting echoes of the town's history in flashes of shadow and light. The disembodied voices, their harmonious chorus resonating with the trio's determination, guided them in weaving a cosmic tapestry that sought to redefine the town's destiny.

Isabella, drawing upon her connection to the supernatural energies, extended her hands toward the entity. The very essence of Ravenshade responded to her touch, sending ripples through the cosmic currents. The entity recoiled, its shape-shifting forms quivering in the face of Isabella's newfound command over the supernatural forces.

The disembodied voices, now a gentle breeze that carried whispers of ancient prophecies, urged Isabella to embrace the town's destiny. Visions of Ravenshade's future played out before her eyes – a future where the supernatural and mortal coexisted in harmony. The cosmic currents responded to her vision, aligning with the tapestry of redemption she sought to weave.

Victor, marked by both the vampiric curse and the ancient energies, stepped forward with a sense of purpose. Memories of centuries past, laden with the weight of his immortal existence, fueled his resolve. The disembodied voices, recognizing Victor's journey of redemption, whispered words of acceptance and transformation.

As Victor confronted the entity, his touch resonated with the cosmic currents. Shadows danced around him, reflecting the struggles of his immortal existence. The disembodied voices, now a supportive presence that echoed through the cosmic winds, guided Victor in channeling the supernatural energies toward a future where Ravenshade could break free from the cyclical curse.

Detective Harris, a mortal navigating the cosmic unknown, faced the shadows of unsolved mysteries with a determination that defied rational explanation. The spectral entities that circled him seemed to waver in the face of his unwavering resolve. The disembodied voices, now a reassuring chant, conveyed that Detective Harris held the key to unraveling the town's enigmas and forging a new path.

The cosmic battle unfolded in a symphony of ethereal energies. The entity, once a formidable manifestation of malevolence, now quivered before the collective resolve of Isabella, Victor, and Detective Harris. The surreal landscape transformed, mirroring their efforts to redefine Ravenshade's destiny.

The disembodied voices, their harmonious melody now a guiding force that resonated through the cosmic currents, urged the trio to unite their strengths. Isabella's connection to the supernatural, Victor's redemption, and Detective Harris's pursuit of truth converged in a powerful synergy. The very fabric of Ravenshade's essence seemed to respond, creating a cosmic equilibrium.

As the trio channeled their collective energy, a radiant glow enveloped them. The spectral entities that had circled them dispersed, dissolving into the cosmic winds. The disembodied voices, now a triumphant anthem, echoed through the surreal realm, heralding a moment of transformation.

Ravenshade's haunting legacy underwent a profound metamorphosis. The very essence of the town pulsed with a revitalized energy. Shadows retreated, and the surreal landscape shifted into a representation of Ravenshade's potential future. The disembodied voices, now a gentle hum that resonated with the town's heartbeat, conveyed a sense of renewal.

Isabella, Victor, and Detective Harris stood at the nexus of Ravenshade's destiny, witnessing the transformation unfold. The entity, once a formidable foe, now dissipated into the cosmic winds, leaving behind a sense of closure and resolution. The surreal landscape settled into a harmonious tableau that reflected the town's newfound equilibrium.

The disembodied voices, their whispers now a comforting presence that echoed through the cosmic currents, conveyed that the cosmic forces had found balance. Ravenshade, freed from the cyclical curse, stood as a beacon of redemption and renewal. The supernatural currents, once a source of malevolence, now flowed with a gentle harmony that resonated through the very fabric of the town.

Isabella, Victor, and Detective Harris, having united their strengths in the cosmic battle, found themselves standing in the moonlit streets of Ravenshade once again. The spectral gateway, now closed, left behind a subtle resonance that hinted at the town's enduring connection to the supernatural. The disembodied voices, their whispers now a distant murmur, conveyed a sense of gratitude and farewell.

The town, now transformed, seemed to exhale a collective sigh of relief. The moon cast a soft glow on the cobblestone streets, and a gentle breeze carried with it the scent of a town reborn. Ravenshade's inhabitants, oblivious to the cosmic drama that had unfolded, slept soundly, their dreams untouched by the haunting legacy that once clung to their town.

Isabella, Victor, and Detective Harris, having played pivotal roles in reshaping Ravenshade's destiny, walked through the moonlit night with a shared sense of accomplishment. The mansion, once a conduit for ancient energies, stood as a testament to the town's resilience and the trio's collective journey.

The disembodied voices, their echoes now a distant memory, conveyed a final message of hope. Ravenshade, once ensnared by a supernatural curse, now stood at the threshold of a new beginning. The trio, having navigated the cosmic currents and confronted the town's darkest fears, left behind a legacy that echoed through the very fabric of Ravenshade's existence.

As dawn approached, the moon dipped below the horizon, casting long shadows on the streets of Ravenshade. The town, now bathed in the soft glow of morning light, seemed to awaken to a new era. The echoes of the supernatural and the triumph of redemption lingered in the air, leaving behind a town that had transcended its haunted history.

Isabella, Victor, and Detective Harris, having played their parts in Ravenshade's transformative journey, watched as the first rays of sunlight kissed the horizon. The town, once a prisoner of its haunting legacy, now embraced a future filled with possibilities. The mansion, standing as a silent witness to the cosmic drama, held the secrets of Ravenshade's past and the promise of a dawn that heralded a new beginning.

Chapter 11: Racing Against Time

The dawn in Ravenshade brought a deceptive calmness, shrouding the town in the gentle embrace of morning light. Isabella, Victor, and Detective Harris, having played pivotal roles in reshaping the town's destiny, found themselves caught in a surreal moment between the cosmic drama and the mundane routines of daily life. Unbeknownst to the townspeople, the very fabric of Ravenshade's existence had undergone a profound transformation.

As the trio navigated the sunlit streets, remnants of the cosmic battle lingered in the air. Shadows danced on the cobblestone pathways, casting fleeting glimpses of spectral entities that seemed to waver at the edge of perception. The mansion, once a conduit for ancient energies, stood as a silent sentinel, its grandeur now stripped of the malevolence that had clung to it for centuries.

Isabella, guided by her connection to the supernatural energies, sensed an underlying current that pulsed beneath the town's surface. The disembodied voices, now a distant murmur that echoed through the cosmic winds, conveyed a sense of vigilance.

Ravenshade, having escaped the cyclical curse, teetered on the brink of a fragile equilibrium between the supernatural and the mundane.

Victor, marked by both the vampiric curse and the ancient energies, grappled with the implications of his newfound connection to the town. Memories of his immortal existence intertwined with visions of a future where Ravenshade embraced a harmonious coexistence. The disembodied voices, recognizing Victor's internal struggle, whispered words of acceptance and a promise of renewal.

Detective Harris, a mortal navigating the cosmic unknown, pondered the implications of the choices made within the surreal realm. The shadows of unsolved mysteries still loomed, their enigmatic presence casting a lingering uncertainty. The disembodied voices, now a gentle breeze that rustled through the morning air, conveyed that Detective Harris held the key to unraveling the town's remaining enigmas.

As the trio delved into their reflections, a subtle unease settled over Ravenshade. The morning breeze carried with it whispers of an ancient prophecy, hinting at the delicate balance that hung over the town's newfound equilibrium. The mansion, its walls now imbued with a solemn calmness, beckoned the trio to explore its halls once more.

Inside the mansion, the atmosphere felt different from the previous night. The grand hall, once a stage for cosmic battles, now exuded a subdued tranquility. The artifact, a centuries-old tapestry that depicted Ravenshade's haunting history, hung on the wall like a silent witness to the town's transformative journey.

Isabella, Victor, and Detective Harris approached the tapestry with a shared sense of curiosity. The woven scenes depicted the town's struggles and triumphs, each thread unraveling a different chapter in Ravenshade's history. The disembodied voices, now a gentle melody that harmonized with the morning breeze, urged the trio to explore the tapestry's hidden truths.

As they studied the artifact, a subtle resonance pulsed through the grand hall. Visions of the surreal realm, the cosmic nexus, and the entity's dissolution played out in spectral flashes within the tapestry. The disembodied voices, now a guiding force that resonated with the threads of fate, conveyed that Ravenshade's destiny remained intertwined with the choices made within the cosmic realm.

The mansion seemed to respond to the trio's presence. Hidden chambers revealed themselves, each holding fragments of Ravenshade's ancient history. Isabella, guided by the whispers of the supernatural, led the exploration. Victor, still marked by the vampiric curse and the ancient energies, sensed a connection to the hidden mysteries within the mansion's walls. Detective Harris, ever the rational investigator, approached each revelation with a cautious curiosity.

In one hidden chamber, a forgotten tome revealed the origin of Ravenshade's haunting legacy. The disembodied voices, their whispers now an ancient chant, conveyed tales of a bygone era where cosmic forces and mortal existence were inseparable. Isabella, Victor, and Detective Harris delved into the tome's pages, unraveling the threads of prophecy that had shaped the town's destiny.

In another chamber, artifacts imbued with supernatural energies hinted at Ravenshade's untold potential. The disembodied voices, now a resonant hum that echoed through the hidden passages, urged the trio to recognize the delicate balance that governed the town's newfound equilibrium. Visions of a future where Ravenshade embraced both the supernatural and the mundane played out in ethereal patterns.

As the trio explored the mansion's secrets, a gradual sense of unease settled over them. Shadows seemed to cling to the edges of perception, and distant whispers carried echoes of an ancient curse that still lingered in the town's essence. The disembodied voices, their gentle melody now a cautionary note, conveyed that Ravenshade's transformative journey was far from over.

Isabella, Victor, and Detective Harris found themselves standing before a sealed chamber, its entrance obscured by a tapestry that depicted a cryptic symbol. The disembodied voices, now a unified chorus that resonated with the threads of fate, conveyed that the answers to Ravenshade's remaining mysteries lay within the chamber's depths.

With a shared sense of determination, the trio unveiled the chamber's entrance. The air within seemed charged with a potent energy, and a sense of trepidation accompanied their steps. The disembodied voices, their whispers now a haunting melody, guided the trio into the heart of Ravenshade's ancient secrets.

As they entered the chamber, the atmosphere shifted. Shadows danced on the walls, and the air seemed to thicken with an otherworldly presence. The disembodied voices, now a foreboding chant that echoed through the chamber, hinted at the ancient curse that still clung to Ravenshade's essence.

Within the chamber's depths, a mysterious artifact lay in the center. The symbol on the tapestry manifested on its surface, pulsating with an ominous glow. Isabella, Victor, and Detective Harris approached the artifact cautiously, sensing that it held the key to unraveling the final mysteries that lingered within Ravenshade.

The disembodied voices, their haunting melody now a spectral chorus, whispered ancient incantations that resonated through the chamber. Visions of the town's cyclical struggles and the spectral entities that had haunted its streets played out around them. The trio felt the weight of Ravenshade's history pressing upon them, a reminder that the ancient curse still held sway over the town.

Isabella, guided by her connection to the supernatural, extended her hands toward the artifact. The disembodied voices, their whispers now urgent and filled with a sense of determination, conveyed that the time had come to confront the remnants of the ancient curse. Shadows within the chamber seemed to converge, forming spectral entities that mirrored the malevolent forces that had plagued Ravenshade for centuries.

As Isabella touched the artifact, the room trembled with a surge of supernatural energy. The symbol on its surface glowed with an intensity that bordered on blinding. The disembodied voices, now a fervent chant that resonated through the chamber's walls, guided Isabella in channeling the cosmic forces to unveil the truth that lay hidden within Ravenshade's essence.

Victor, marked by the vampiric curse and the ancient energies, felt a resonance with the artifact. Memories of his immortal existence intertwined with the currents of supernatural power that emanated from the symbol. The disembodied voices, recognizing Victor's pivotal role in the town's transformative journey, urged him to confront the shadows of his own past.

Detective Harris, a mortal caught in the cosmic currents, observed the unfolding scene with a sense of wary vigilance. The spectral entities within the chamber seemed to respond to his presence, their shapes contorting with an eerie sentience. The disembodied voices, now a cautionary whisper, conveyed that Detective Harris held the key to unraveling the town's remaining enigmas.

Together, the trio channeled their collective energies into the artifact. The symbol on its surface wavered, revealing glimpses of an ethereal realm where the cosmic forces and mortal existence converged. The disembodied voices, their spectral chorus now a harmonic blend of warning and guidance, urged the trio to navigate the ancient curse's final remnants.

As the chamber resonated with supernatural energy, a spectral gateway opened before them. Visions of Ravenshade's haunted history played out within the gateway, each scene a reflection of the town's struggles and triumphs. The disembodied voices, now a swirling tempest of guidance, conveyed that the trio needed to step through the gateway to confront the ancient curse at its source.

Isabella, Victor, and Detective Harris entered the spectral gateway, finding themselves in a surreal realm where the echoes of Ravenshade's history converged. The disembodied voices, now a haunting melody that reverberated through the cosmic winds, guided them toward a distant horizon where the remnants of the ancient curse awaited.

The landscape within the spectral realm shifted between ethereal manifestations of Ravenshade's past and present. Shadows danced with an eerie sentience, forming spectral entities that seemed to embody the malevolent forces that had plagued the town. The disembodied voices, their spectral chorus now a foreboding anthem, urged the trio to confront the shadows that clung to Ravenshade's essence.

As they moved through the spectral realm, the very fabric of reality seemed to warp around them. The disembodied voices, now a cacophony of haunting whispers, revealed fragments of the ancient curse's origin. Ravenshade, it seemed, had been bound by a cosmic balance that teetered between redemption and descent into a darker unknown.

The trio reached the nexus where the remnants of the ancient curse manifested. A shadowy figure, cloaked in ethereal energies, stood at the center. The disembodied voices, now a mournful dirge that echoed through the spectral winds, conveyed that this figure embodied the collective fears and struggles of Ravenshade.

Isabella, Victor, and Detective Harris confronted the shadowy figure with a shared sense of determination. The disembodied voices, their haunting melody now an anthem of defiance, urged the trio to channel the cosmic forces and break the ancient curse's final hold on the town.

A surreal battle unfolded within the spectral realm. Shadows clashed, and echoes of Ravenshade's history played out in ethereal flashes. The disembodied voices, their spectral chorus now a triumphant symphony, guided the trio in weaving a cosmic tapestry that sought to sever the town's connection to the ancient curse.

Isabella, drawing upon her connection to the supernatural energies, reached into the very fabric of Ravenshade's essence. The shadowy figure recoiled, its ethereal form quivering in the face of Isabella's newfound command over the cosmic forces. The disembodied voices, now a harmonious melody that resonated with the threads of fate, conveyed that Isabella's choice had the power to redefine the town's destiny.

Victor, marked by both the vampiric curse and the ancient energies, confronted the shadowy figure with a newfound understanding. His immortal existence, once a source of isolation, became a conduit for transformation. The disembodied voices, recognizing Victor's journey of redemption, whispered words of acceptance and a promise of renewal.

Detective Harris, a mortal navigating the cosmic unknown, faced the shadows of unsolved mysteries with a determination that defied rational explanation. The spectral entities that circled him seemed to waver in the face of his unwavering resolve. The disembodied voices, now a supportive presence that echoed through the spectral winds, conveyed that Detective Harris held the key to unraveling the town's remaining enigmas.

As the trio channeled their collective energy, a radiant glow enveloped them. The spectral entities that had circled them dissipated, dissolving into the cosmic winds. The disembodied voices, their ethereal chorus now a resolute anthem, echoed through the spectral realm, heralding a moment of transformation.

The ancient curse, its remnants dispersed in the spectral winds, lifted from Ravenshade's essence. The surreal landscape settled into a harmonious tableau that reflected the town's newfound equilibrium. The disembodied voices, their haunting melody now a soothing lullaby, conveyed that Ravenshade's destiny had been rewritten.

Isabella, Victor, and Detective Harris found themselves standing at the nexus of Ravenshade's transformed destiny. The shadowy figure, once a formidable manifestation of malevolence, now dissipated into the cosmic winds, leaving behind a sense of closure and resolution. The surreal landscape shifted, mirroring the town's newfound

harmony. The disembodied voices, their whispers now a gentle breeze that caressed the spectral winds, conveyed a sense of gratitude and farewell.

As the trio emerged from the spectral realm, they found themselves back in the mansion, the artifacts and hidden chambers now bathed in a serene glow. Ravenshade's haunting legacy had been vanquished, and the town stood at the threshold of a new beginning.

The disembodied voices, their echoes now a distant memory, conveyed a final message of hope and redemption. Ravenshade, once ensnared by an ancient curse, now embraced a future where the supernatural and the mundane coexisted in harmony. The mansion, standing as a silent witness to the cosmic drama, held the secrets of Ravenshade's past and the promise of a dawn that heralded a new era.

The sun dipped below the horizon, casting long shadows on the streets of Ravenshade. The town, now bathed in the soft glow of twilight, seemed to exhale a collective sigh of relief. The supernatural currents, once a source of malevolence, now flowed with a gentle harmony that resonated through the very fabric of the town.

Isabella, Victor, and Detective Harris walked through the tranquil streets with a shared sense of accomplishment. The townspeople, unaware of the cosmic battles that had unfolded, went about their lives in blissful ignorance. The mansion, its grandeur now stripped of the haunting energies, stood as a testament to the town's resilience.

Days turned into weeks, and Ravenshade embraced its transformed destiny. The mansion, once a focal point of supernatural energies, became a symbol of the town's triumph over ancient curses. The disembodied voices, their whispers now a distant echo in Ravenshade's history, conveyed that the cosmic forces had found balance, and the town had become a beacon of redemption.

Isabella and Victor, having played pivotal roles in Ravenshade's transformative journey, found solace in each other's company. The bond forged through the trials of the cosmic realm deepened into a connection that transcended the supernatural. The mansion, now a haven for the couple, echoed with the laughter and warmth of newfound love.

Detective Harris, having confronted the shadows of unsolved mysteries, continued his role as the town's protector. The remnants of the supernatural no longer haunted Ravenshade, but Detective Harris remained vigilant, ensuring the safety and tranquility of the townspeople. The mansion, once a place of enigma, became a symbol of justice and order.

As the seasons changed, Ravenshade blossomed into a town reborn. The supernatural currents, once a malevolent force, became an integral part of the town's charm. The mansion, standing proud on the edge of town, became a historical landmark, its walls holding the secrets of a transformative journey.

The disembodied voices, their echoes now a fading memory, left Ravenshade with a sense of gratitude. The town, having faced the brink of darkness, emerged into the light of a new beginning. The mansion's halls, once filled with eerie whispers, now resonated with the laughter and joy of Ravenshade's inhabitants.

Years passed, and Ravenshade's haunting history became a distant tale. The mansion, with its storied past, remained a testament to the town's resilience and triumph over supernatural forces. Isabella, Victor, and Detective Harris, though their roles in the transformative journey had become legends, found peace in knowing that Ravenshade had transcended its haunted legacy.

The town, now a harmonious blend of the supernatural and the mundane, continued to thrive. The mansion, once a focal point of cosmic struggles, stood as a beacon of redemption. The disembodied voices, now a gentle breeze that carried the whispers of Ravenshade's past, conveyed that the town's destiny had been rewritten, and a new chapter had begun.

And so, Ravenshade, once ensnared by the shadows of an ancient curse, embraced a future where the echoes of the cosmic realm faded into the annals of history. The mansion, with its imposing presence, stood as a guardian of the town's transformative journey, a silent reminder that even in the face of darkness, redemption and renewal were possible.

Chapter 12: The Pact

In the dimly lit chambers of Ravenshade's ancient mansion, a lingering unease settled over Isabella, Victor, and Detective Harris. The transformative journey they had undertaken seemed far from over as mysterious occurrences began to unfold within the town's historic walls.

As night descended upon Ravenshade, shadows played tricks on the walls of the mansion. Creaking floorboards echoed through the grand halls, carrying whispers of a past that refused to fade away. Isabella, guided by her connection to the supernatural, felt a subtle disturbance in the cosmic energies that lingered within the mansion's labyrinthine corridors.

The disembodied voices, once a comforting presence, now seemed to echo with a sense of urgency. Isabella, Victor, and Detective Harris gathered in the grand hall, their senses heightened by the mysterious energy that permeated the air. A tapestry on the wall, depicting Ravenshade's history, flickered with spectral lights as if harboring secrets waiting to be unveiled.

Detective Harris, the rational investigator amidst the supernatural, examined the tapestry. His keen eyes noticed subtle shifts in the woven scenes – scenes that hinted at a dark force awakening within the mansion. The disembodied voices, now a murmur that rode the evening breeze, urged the trio to delve deeper into the mysteries that clung to Ravenshade's legacy.

In the flickering candlelight, Isabella revealed that ancient prophecies foretold of a dormant malevolence within the mansion. A force that had once been subdued was now stirring, its spectral tendrils reaching out to intertwine with the town's destiny. The disembodied voices, their whispers now tinged with concern, conveyed that Ravenshade stood at the precipice of a new, more ominous chapter.

As the trio ventured further into the mansion's depths, the atmosphere thickened with an otherworldly tension. Portraits lining the walls seemed to follow their every move, their eyes flickering with an unsettling luminosity. The disembodied voices, now an eerie hum that resonated through the halls, guided the trio toward a hidden chamber that held the key to unraveling the looming darkness.

The chamber, concealed behind a tapestry bearing the same cryptic symbol encountered before, revealed itself with a slow, ominous creak. Isabella, Victor, and Detective Harris entered cautiously, the air inside laden with an oppressive energy. The room seemed frozen in time, relics from centuries past arranged with an unsettling precision.

In the center of the chamber, an ancient artifact pulsated with an otherworldly glow. The symbol etched upon it radiated with an intensity that sent shivers down the trio's spines. The disembodied voices, their whispers now a haunting chant, conveyed that the artifact held the essence of the dormant malevolence, waiting to be awakened.

As Isabella reached out to touch the artifact, a surge of supernatural energy coursed through the room. Visions of Ravenshade's darkest moments played out like ghostly projections, each scene more unsettling than the last. The disembodied voices, now a chorus of lament, echoed the collective fear and sorrow embedded within the town's history.

Victor, marked by the vampiric curse and the ancient energies, felt a resonance with the malevolence that stirred within the artifact. Memories of his immortal existence intertwined with the spectral tendrils, revealing glimpses of a time when the mansion was a nexus for unspeakable darkness. The disembodied voices, recognizing Victor's connection to the ancient forces, whispered warnings of a looming threat.

Detective Harris, ever the pragmatic investigator, examined the artifact with a cautious scrutiny. The room seemed to respond to his presence, shadows converging with an eerie sentience. The disembodied voices, now a dissonant melody that echoed through the chamber, conveyed that Detective Harris held the key to unlocking the mysteries and preventing the malevolence from resurfacing.

As the trio grappled with the supernatural forces that surrounded them, the mansion's grand hall echoed with spectral whispers. The tapestry, once a depiction of Ravenshade's history, now seemed to weave a narrative of impending doom. The disembodied voices, their ethereal chorus now a dirge, warned of a formidable adversary that sought to reawaken within the town's historic walls.

The trio, guided by the haunting melodies of the disembodied voices, embarked on a perilous journey to uncover the mansion's darkest secrets. Hidden passages revealed forgotten chambers, each holding fragments of the malevolence that had been sealed away for centuries. The mansion seemed to breathe with a life of its own, shadows dancing with an unsettling sentience.

In their quest for answers, Isabella, Victor, and Detective Harris stumbled upon an ancient tome hidden within the mansion's library. The pages whispered of an age-old ritual used to suppress the malevolence that lurked within the artifact. The disembodied voices, now a desperate plea that resonated through the chamber, urged the trio to perform the ritual before the malevolence could fully awaken.

The ritual required the combined strengths of Isabella, Victor, and Detective Harris. Symbols were etched, incantations chanted, and the very fabric of supernatural energy manipulated to seal away the malevolence once more. The mansion seemed to resist, its walls echoing with disembodied screams and whispers that sought to break the trio's resolve.

As the ritual reached its crescendo, a surge of malevolent energy lashed out. Shadows within the chamber took form, coalescing into a spectral entity that mirrored the darkness they sought to suppress. The disembodied voices, their haunting chorus now a desperate cry, guided the trio in a final push to complete the ritual.

The room trembled with the cosmic forces at play, the tapestry on the wall flickering with spectral lights. Isabella, Victor, and Detective Harris stood united against the malevolence that sought to consume Ravenshade. The disembodied voices, their ethereal melody now a triumphant anthem, conveyed that the ritual had succeeded in subduing the ancient threat.

As the malevolence retreated, the mansion's atmosphere shifted. The shadows that had clung to the walls dissipated, and an eerie calm settled over the hidden chamber. The disembodied voices, their echoes now a soothing hum, conveyed a sense of relief. Ravenshade, once again, had narrowly escaped the clutches of its haunted past.

Isabella, Victor, and Detective Harris emerged from the hidden chamber, the mansion's grand hall now bathed in a serene light. The tapestry on the wall, once a source of spectral disturbances, now hung in stillness. The disembodied voices, their whispers now a gentle breeze that carried through the mansion, conveyed a sense of gratitude and farewell.

The trio, having faced the malevolence that lurked within Ravenshade's historic walls, walked through the moonlit streets with a shared sense of accomplishment. The town, oblivious to the supernatural battles that had unfolded, slept soundly as if the malevolence had never stirred. The mansion, standing as a silent sentinel on the edge of town, held the secrets of a narrowly averted catastrophe.

The disembodied voices, their echoes now a distant memory, left Ravenshade with a final message of caution. The town, though temporarily free from the malevolence, still bore the scars of its haunting legacy. Isabella, Victor, and Detective Harris, having played their parts in preserving Ravenshade's delicate equilibrium, found themselves on the precipice of a new chapter –

Chapter 13: Desperate Measures

In the aftermath of their encounter with the malevolence within the mansion, Ravenshade bore a lingering unease. Isabella, Victor, and Detective Harris, though victorious in subduing the ancient threat, sensed that the town's supernatural currents remained unsettled. Whispers of an impending darkness lingered in the air.

As nightfall cloaked Ravenshade, the mansion's grand halls seemed to echo with the residual energy of the malevolence. Shadows danced on the walls, and the air carried a chilling weight. The disembodied voices, once a comforting presence, now reverberated with an ominous undertone, hinting at an encroaching menace.

Isabella, guided by her connection to the supernatural, felt a lingering disturbance in the cosmic energies that permeated the town. The tapestry on the wall, once a silent witness to Ravenshade's history, seemed to flicker with spectral lights, conveying a message that the malevolence they had subdued might not be fully vanquished. The disembodied voices, their whispers now a cautionary murmur, urged the trio to remain vigilant.

Detective Harris, grappling with the shadows of unsolved mysteries, approached the unfolding events with a sense of wary vigilance. The mansion, once a bastion of supernatural energies, now stood as a potential epicenter of a looming threat. The disembodied voices, now a dissonant melody that rode the evening breeze, conveyed that Detective Harris held the key to uncovering the town's remaining enigmas.

Victor, marked by both the vampiric curse and the ancient energies, felt a resonance with the lingering malevolence. Memories of his immortal existence intertwined with the subtle shifts in the town's essence. The disembodied voices, recognizing Victor's unique connection to the supernatural, whispered forewarnings of an imminent darkness that sought to envelop Ravenshade.

As the trio delved deeper into the mansion's mysteries, hidden chambers revealed themselves once more. The artifact, though seemingly dormant, pulsed with a residual energy that hinted at an unfulfilled purpose. The disembodied voices, now an urgent whisper that echoed through the hidden passages, conveyed that Ravenshade's destiny teetered on the edge of a perilous precipice.

In their quest for answers, Isabella, Victor, and Detective Harris discovered an ancient tome that detailed the cyclical nature of malevolence within the mansion. The disembodied voices, their whispers now a haunting chant, revealed that the malevolence had been temporarily subdued but not eradicated. The town's delicate equilibrium hung in the balance, and the trio faced the daunting task of preventing the ancient threat from resurfacing.

Symbols were etched, incantations chanted, as the trio performed rituals to strengthen the mystical wards that guarded Ravenshade. The mansion seemed to resist, its walls echoing with disembodied screams and whispers that sought to break the trio's resolve. The disembodied voices, their ethereal chorus now a desperate cry, guided the trio in a final push to fortify the town against the encroaching darkness.

The rituals, though potent, revealed glimpses of a malevolent force attempting to breach the supernatural barriers. Shadows within the mansion seemed to writhe with an unnatural sentience, and the disembodied voices, their spectral chorus now a dirge, conveyed that Ravenshade's defenses were being tested by an ancient adversary that sought retribution.

As the trio stood united against the looming threat, a surge of malevolent energy lashed out. Shadows within the mansion converged into a spectral entity that mirrored the darkness they sought to repel. The disembodied voices, their haunting melody now a symphony of resistance, guided the trio in a final stand against the encroaching malevolence.

The mansion trembled with the cosmic forces at play, the tapestry on the wall flickering with spectral lights. Isabella, Victor, and Detective Harris, bound by a shared determination, confronted the malevolent force with an unwavering resolve. The disembodied voices, their ethereal chorus now a triumphant anthem, conveyed that the town's destiny rested on the trio's ability to thwart the impending darkness.

A surreal battle unfolded within the mansion's grand halls. Shadows clashed, and echoes of Ravenshade's history played out in ethereal flashes. The disembodied voices, their spectral chorus now a rallying cry, guided the trio in weaving a cosmic tapestry that sought to repel the malevolence seeking to envelop the town.

Isabella, drawing upon her connection to the supernatural energies, reached into the very fabric of Ravenshade's essence. The spectral entity recoiled, its ethereal form quivering in the face of Isabella's newfound command over the cosmic forces. The disembodied voices, recognizing Isabella's pivotal role in the town's transformative journey, whispered words of empowerment and a promise of resilience.

Victor, marked by the vampiric curse and the ancient energies, confronted the spectral entity with a newfound understanding. His immortal existence, once a source of isolation, became a beacon of resistance against the encroaching darkness. The disembodied voices, recognizing Victor's journey of redemption, echoed a chorus of support and encouragement.

Detective Harris, a mortal navigating the cosmic unknown, faced the shadows with a determination that defied rational explanation. The spectral entity seemed to waver in the face of his unwavering resolve. The disembodied voices, now a supportive presence that echoed through the spectral winds, conveyed that Detective Harris held the key to fortifying Ravenshade's defenses.

As the trio channeled their collective energy, a radiant glow enveloped them. The spectral entity, unable to withstand the unified resistance, dissipated into the cosmic winds. The disembodied voices, their ethereal chorus now a resolute anthem, echoed through the mansion, heralding a moment of renewed strength.

Ravenshade, once again, emerged from the brink of darkness. The mansion's grand halls, though marked by the cosmic battles, now stood as a testament to the town's resilience. The disembodied voices, their whispers now a gentle breeze that carried through the mansion, conveyed a sense of gratitude and farewell.

Isabella, Victor, and Detective Harris, having faced the malevolence that sought to engulf Ravenshade, walked through the moonlit streets with a shared sense of accomplishment. The

Chapter 14: Love Conquers All

Amidst the eerie calm that settled over Ravenshade after the confrontation with the malevolence, a disquieting unease lingered in the air. Isabella, Victor, and Detective Harris, although successful in fortifying the town's defenses, sensed that the supernatural currents were far from tranquil. Whispers of an impending threat echoed through the mansion's grand halls.

Nightfall draped the town in shadows, and the mansion seemed to hold its breath as if anticipating a malevolent force lurking in the unseen. The disembodied voices, once a comforting presence, now hinted at a spectral tension, suggesting that the recent victory might have only momentarily subdued the cosmic turmoil within Ravenshade.

Isabella, with her innate connection to the supernatural, felt a lingering disturbance in the cosmic energies. The tapestry on the wall, a silent witness to the town's history, flickered with spectral lights, conveying a cryptic message that foretold of an unresolved darkness. The disembodied voices, now a murmur tinged with urgency, urged the trio to delve deeper into the mysteries that clung to Ravenshade's legacy.

Detective Harris, ever vigilant, approached the unfolding events with a watchful eye. The mansion, once a focal point of supernatural energies, now stood as a potential epicenter for an impending threat. The disembodied voices, now a dissonant melody carried by the evening breeze, conveyed that Detective Harris held the key to uncovering the town's remaining enigmas.

Victor, marked by both the vampiric curse and the ancient energies, felt an unsettling resonance in the air. Memories of his immortal existence intertwined with the subtle shifts in the town's essence. The disembodied voices, recognizing Victor's unique connection to the supernatural, whispered forewarnings of an imminent darkness that sought to envelop Ravenshade once more.

As the trio navigated the mansion's shadow-laden corridors, hidden chambers revealed themselves, each echoing with the residual energy of the malevolence. The artifact, seemingly dormant, pulsated with a lingering power that hinted at an unfulfilled purpose. The disembodied voices, now an urgent whisper echoing through the hidden passages, conveyed that Ravenshade's destiny teetered on the edge of a perilous precipice.

In their quest for answers, Isabella, Victor, and Detective Harris uncovered an ancient tome that detailed the cyclical nature of malevolence within the mansion. The disembodied voices, their whispers now a haunting chant, revealed that the malevolence had been temporarily subdued but not eradicated. The town's delicate equilibrium hung in the balance, and the trio faced the daunting task of preventing the ancient threat from resurfacing.

Symbols were etched, incantations chanted, as the trio performed rituals to strengthen the mystical wards that guarded Ravenshade. The mansion seemed to resist, its walls echoing with disembodied screams and whispers that sought to break the trio's resolve. The disembodied voices, their ethereal chorus now a desperate cry, guided the trio in a final push to fortify the town against the encroaching darkness.

The rituals, though potent, revealed glimpses of a malevolent force attempting to breach the supernatural barriers. Shadows within the mansion seemed to writhe with an unnatural sentience, and the disembodied voices, their spectral chorus now a dirge, conveyed that Ravenshade's defenses were being tested by an ancient adversary that sought retribution.

As the trio stood united against the looming threat, a surge of malevolent energy lashed out. Shadows within the mansion converged into a spectral entity that mirrored the darkness they sought to repel. The disembodied voices, their haunting melody now a symphony of resistance, guided the trio in a final stand against the encroaching malevolence.

The mansion trembled with the cosmic forces at play, the tapestry on the wall flickering with spectral lights. Isabella, Victor, and Detective Harris, bound by a shared determination, confronted the malevolent force with an unwavering resolve. The disembodied voices, their ethereal chorus now a triumphant anthem, conveyed that the town's destiny rested on the trio's ability to thwart the impending darkness.

A surreal battle unfolded within the mansion's grand halls. Shadows clashed, and echoes of Ravenshade's history played out in ethereal flashes. The disembodied voices, their spectral chorus now a rallying cry, guided the trio in weaving a cosmic tapestry that sought to repel the malevolence seeking to envelop the town.

Isabella, drawing upon her connection to the supernatural energies, reached into the very fabric of Ravenshade's essence. The spectral entity recoiled, its ethereal form quivering in the face of Isabella's newfound command over the cosmic forces. The disembodied voices, recognizing Isabella's pivotal role in the town's transformative journey, whispered words of empowerment and a promise of resilience.

Victor, marked by the vampiric curse and the ancient energies, confronted the spectral entity with a newfound understanding. His immortal existence, once a source of isolation, became a beacon of resistance against the encroaching darkness. The disembodied voices, recognizing Victor's journey of redemption, echoed a chorus of support and encouragement.

Detective Harris, a mortal navigating the cosmic unknown, faced the shadows with a determination that defied rational explanation. The spectral entity seemed to waver in the face of his unwavering resolve. The disembodied voices, now a supportive presence that echoed through the spectral winds, conveyed that Detective Harris held the key to fortifying Ravenshade's defenses.

As the trio channeled their collective energy, a radiant glow enveloped them. The spectral entity, unable to withstand the unified resistance, dissipated into the cosmic winds. The disembodied voices, their ethereal chorus now a resolute anthem, echoed through the mansion, heralding a moment of renewed strength.

Ravenshade, once again, emerged from the brink of darkness. The mansion's grand halls, though marked by the cosmic battles, now stood as a testament to the town's resilience. The disembodied voices, their whispers now a gentle breeze that carried through the mansion, conveyed a sense of gratitude and farewell.

Isabella, Victor, and Detective Harris, having faced the malevolence that sought to engulf Ravenshade, walked through the moonlit streets with a shared sense of accomplishment. The town, though temporarily free from the malevolence, still bore the scars of its haunting legacy. The mansion, standing as a silent sentinel on the edge of town, held the secrets of a narrowly averted catastrophe.

The disembodied voices, their echoes now a distant memory, left Ravenshade with a final message of caution. The town, though momentarily spared, remained intertwined with the supernatural currents that flowed beneath its surface. Isabella, Victor, and Detective Harris, having played their parts in preserving Ravenshade's delicate equilibrium, found themselves on the precipice of a new chapter − a chapter that would test their resilience in the face of an ever-evolving cosmic tapestry.

Days turned into weeks, and Ravenshade, seemingly restored to tranquility, carried the echoes of its supernatural battles. The mansion's grand halls, once the stage for cosmic confrontations, now stood as a symbol of the town's endurance. The disembodied voices, though silent, left an indelible imprint on Ravenshade's history, a testament to the intertwined destinies of the supernatural and the mundane.

Yet, as the trio sought solace in the newfound peace, a subtle undercurrent hinted at the fragility of their triumph. Isabella, in her moments of quiet reflection, detected faint ripples in the cosmic energies. The tapestry on the wall, though still, seemed to hold a spectral resonance that whispered of untold secrets. The disembodied voices, though dormant, left an unsettling sense that Ravenshade's journey was far from over.

Detective Harris, resuming his role as the town's protector, delved into the unsolved mysteries that lingered in the shadows. The mansion, once a font of malevolence, now harbored unanswered questions. The disembodied voices, their whispers now a spectral echo, guided Detective Harris toward forgotten corners of Ravenshade where the threads of the supernatural wove a complex tapestry.

Victor, haunted by his vampiric past, grappled with the residue of the malevolence that clung to his immortal existence. The mansion, once a nexus of darkness, now stood as a reflection of his journey toward redemption. The disembodied voices, their ethereal echoes now a companion to Victor's solitude, hinted at the intricacies of his intertwined fate with Ravenshade.

As the days unfolded, subtle disturbances hinted at an encroaching cosmic disturbance. Strange occurrences, seemingly benign at first, rippled through Ravenshade. Objects moved on their own accord, and spectral whispers lingered in the stillness of the night. The disembodied voices, though subdued, murmured warnings that the town's newfound peace was a fragile balance on the edge of unraveling.

Isabella, sensing the shifting energies, convened with Victor and Detective Harris. The mansion's grand hall, once witness to cosmic battles, now served as a council chamber. The disembodied voices, their whispers now a cautious counsel, conveyed that Ravenshade faced a new challenge – a threat that sought to exploit the town's supernatural vulnerabilities.

The trio, bound by their shared history, embarked on a renewed quest to safeguard Ravenshade. The mansion's hidden chambers, once sealed, revealed new enigmas that intertwined with the ancient forces at play. The disembodied voices, their spectral presence now a guiding light, urged Isabella, Victor, and Detective Harris to unravel the mysteries that unfolded within the town's historic walls.

As the cosmic tapestry of Ravenshade's fate unfolded, the trio discovered forgotten rituals and untapped powers that could fortify the town against the encroaching darkness. Symbols were etched, incantations recited, as the mansion once again became a focal point for supernatural battles. The disembodied voices, though subdued, harmonized with the trio's efforts, guiding them in their renewed struggle to protect the delicate balance between the realms.

The mansion, now a bastion of both ancient curses and new-found strengths, echoed with the sounds of cosmic confrontation. Shadows danced on the walls, and the tapestry on the wall seemed to writhe with spectral energies. The disembodied voices, their echoes now a melodic chant, resonated through Ravenshade as a harbinger of the challenges that lay ahead.

Days turned into nights, and the town once again found itself on the edge of a cosmic precipice. Isabella, Victor, and Detective Harris, united by a common purpose, faced the unfolding darkness with a resilience forged in the crucible of supernatural battles. The mansion, with its grandeur now a canvas for the struggles of the supernatural, stood as a sentinel on the outskirts of town, its walls holding the secrets of Ravenshade's enduring journey through the realms of the unknown.

Chapter 15: The Final Clue

Amidst the fragile peace that Ravenshade had momentarily embraced, an unsettling undercurrent pulsed through the town. Isabella, Victor, and Detective Harris sensed a renewed cosmic disturbance, a stirring in the supernatural currents that hinted at an approaching malevolence. Whispers of spectral threats lingered, and the mansion's grand halls seemed to shiver with an eerie anticipation.

As night descended upon Ravenshade, shadows once again played tricks on the walls of the mansion. The tapestry on the wall, once a silent observer, now flickered with spectral lights, conveying an ominous message that the town's respite was but a fleeting illusion. The disembodied voices, their whispers now tinged with urgency, guided the trio to confront a new and formidable adversary.

Isabella, attuned to the cosmic energies, felt a disturbance in the air that transcended the mundane. The town, once bathed in the glow of temporary tranquility, now harbored a darkness that sought to unravel the delicate threads of balance. The disembodied voices, their spectral echoes now a haunting refrain, warned that Ravenshade's destiny was at the mercy of an ancient force eager to exploit its supernatural vulnerabilities.

Detective Harris, ever the pragmatic investigator, sensed a shift in the town's atmosphere. The mansion, once a repository of mysteries, now stood as a battleground between the mundane and the supernatural. The disembodied voices, their whispers now a dissonant melody carried by the night breeze, conveyed that Detective Harris held the key to unlocking the town's defenses against the encroaching malevolence.

Victor, marked by the vampiric curse and the ancient energies, felt the ominous resonance in his immortal bones. The mansion, once a vessel of redemption, now pulsated with a darkness that mirrored his haunted past. The disembodied voices, recognizing

Victor's enduring struggle, whispered forewarnings of a malevolence that sought to entwine itself with his immortal existence.

As the trio ventured into the mansion's labyrinthine corridors, hidden chambers revealed new secrets. The artifact, once seemingly subdued, resonated with a malevolent energy that sought release. The disembodied voices, now an urgent whisper echoing through the hidden passages, conveyed that Ravenshade stood on the precipice of a new and perilous chapter.

In their quest for answers, Isabella, Victor, and Detective Harris discovered ancient prophecies foretelling of a cosmic convergence that would test the very fabric of Ravenshade's existence. The disembodied voices, their whispers now a haunting chant, revealed that the town's destiny was intertwined with a malevolence that had lurked in the shadows since time immemorial.

Symbols were etched, incantations chanted, as the trio performed rituals to fortify Ravenshade against the impending darkness. The mansion seemed to resist, its walls echoing with disembodied screams and whispers that sought to break the trio's resolve. The disembodied voices, their ethereal chorus now a desperate cry, guided the trio in a final push to shield the town from the encroaching malevolence.

The rituals, though potent, unveiled glimpses of a malevolent force attempting to breach the supernatural barriers. Shadows within the mansion writhed with an unnatural sentience, and the disembodied voices, their spectral chorus now a dirge, conveyed that Ravenshade's defenses were under siege by an ancient adversary seeking retribution.

As the trio stood united against the looming threat, a surge of malevolent energy lashed out. Shadows within the mansion converged into a spectral entity that mirrored the darkness they sought to repel. The disembodied voices, their haunting melody now a symphony of resistance, guided the trio in a final stand against the encroaching malevolence.

The mansion trembled with the cosmic forces at play, the tapestry on the wall flickering with spectral lights. Isabella, Victor, and Detective Harris, bound by a shared determination, confronted the malevolent force with unwavering resolve. The disembodied voices, their ethereal chorus now a triumphant anthem, conveyed that the town's destiny rested on the trio's ability to thwart the impending darkness.

A surreal battle unfolded within the mansion's grand halls. Shadows clashed, and echoes of Ravenshade's history played out in ethereal flashes. The disembodied voices, their spectral chorus now a rallying cry, guided the trio in weaving a cosmic tapestry that sought to repel the malevolence seeking to envelop the town.

Isabella, drawing upon her connection to the supernatural energies, reached into the very fabric of Ravenshade's essence. The spectral entity recoiled, its ethereal form quivering in the face of Isabella's newfound command over the cosmic forces. The disembodied voices, recognizing Isabella's pivotal role in the town's transformative journey, whispered words of empowerment and a promise of resilience.

Victor, marked by the vampiric curse and the ancient energies, confronted the spectral entity with a newfound understanding. His immortal existence, once a source of isolation, became a beacon of resistance against the encroaching darkness. The disembodied voices, recognizing Victor's journey of redemption, echoed a chorus of support and encouragement.

Detective Harris, a mortal navigating the cosmic unknown, faced the shadows with a determination that defied rational explanation. The spectral entity seemed to waver in the face of his unwavering resolve. The disembodied voices, now a supportive presence that echoed through the spectral winds, conveyed that Detective Harris held the key to fortifying Ravenshade's defenses.

As the trio channeled their collective energy, a radiant glow enveloped them. The spectral entity, unable to withstand the unified resistance, dissipated into the cosmic winds. The disembodied voices, their ethereal chorus now a resolute anthem, echoed through the mansion, heralding a moment of triumph over the encroaching malevolence.

Ravenshade, once again, emerged from the brink of darkness. The mansion's grand halls, though marked by the cosmic battles, now stood as a testament to the town's resilience. The disembodied voices, their whispers now a gentle breeze that carried through the mansion, conveyed a sense of gratitude and farewell.

Isabella, Victor, and Detective Harris, having faced the malevolence that sought to engulf Ravenshade, walked through the moonlit streets with a shared sense of accomplishment. The town, though battered by the cosmic storms, bore the scars of its battles with newfound strength. The mansion, standing stoically on the edge of town, seemed to exhale a sigh of relief.

The disembodied voices, their echoes now a distant memory, left Ravenshade with a final message of caution. The town, though momentarily spared, remained intertwined with the supernatural currents that flowed beneath its surface. Isabella, Victor, and Detective Harris, having played their parts in preserving Ravenshade's delicate equilibrium, found themselves on the precipice of a new chapter – a chapter that would test their resilience in the face of an ever-evolving cosmic tapestry.

Days turned into weeks, and Ravenshade, seemingly restored to tranquility, carried the echoes of its supernatural battles. The mansion's grand halls, once the stage for cosmic confrontations, now stood as a symbol of the town's endurance. The disembodied voices, though silent, left an indelible imprint on Ravenshade's history, a testament to the intertwined destinies of the supernatural and the mundane.

Yet, as the trio sought solace in the newfound peace, a subtle undercurrent hinted at the fragility of their triumph. Isabella, in her moments of quiet reflection, detected faint ripples in the cosmic energies. The tapestry on the wall, though still, seemed to hold a spectral resonance that whispered of untold secrets. The disembodied voices, though dormant, left an unsettling sense that Ravenshade's journey was far from over.

Detective Harris, resuming his role as the town's protector, delved into the unsolved mysteries that lingered in the shadows. The mansion, once a font of malevolence, now harbored unanswered questions. The disembodied voices, their whispers now a spectral echo, guided Detective Harris toward forgotten corners of Ravenshade where the threads of the supernatural wove a complex tapestry.

Victor, haunted by his vampiric past, grappled with the residue of the malevolence that clung to his immortal existence. The mansion, once a nexus of darkness, now stood as a reflection of his journey toward redemption. The disembodied voices, their ethereal echoes now a companion to Victor's solitude, hinted at the intricacies of his intertwined fate with Ravenshade.

As the days unfolded, subtle disturbances hinted at an encroaching cosmic disturbance. Strange occurrences, seemingly benign at first, rippled through Ravenshade. Objects moved on their own accord, and spectral whispers lingered in the stillness of the night. The disembodied voices, though subdued, murmured warnings that the town's newfound peace was a fragile balance on the edge of unraveling.

Isabella, sensing the shifting energies, convened with Victor and Detective Harris. The mansion's grand hall, once witness to cosmic battles, now served as a council chamber. The disembodied voices, their whispers now a cautious counsel, conveyed that Ravenshade faced a new challenge – a threat that sought to exploit the town's supernatural vulnerabilities.

The trio, bound by their shared history, embarked on a renewed quest to safeguard Ravenshade. The mansion's hidden chambers, once sealed, revealed new enigmas that intertwined with the ancient forces at play. The disembodied voices, though subdued, harmonized with the trio's efforts, guiding them in their renewed struggle to protect the delicate balance between the realms.

The mansion, now a bastion of both ancient curses and new-found strengths, echoed with the sounds of cosmic confrontation. Shadows danced on the walls, and the tapestry on the wall seemed to writhe with spectral energies. The disembodied voices, though subdued, murmured warnings through the ethereal winds, cautioning the trio that Ravenshade's journey through the realms of the unknown was far from over.

Chapter 16: The Chase

Within the hallowed halls of the mansion, a disconcerting quiet settled over Ravenshade. Isabella, Victor, and Detective Harris could feel the weight of an impending darkness, a palpable tension that hung in the air. The once-tranquil town now carried the burden of an unresolved malevolence, casting an eerie shadow over its streets.

As night descended, the mansion's grand halls echoed with ominous creaks and whispers. The tapestry on the wall, a silent witness to the town's history, seemed to come alive with unsettling images. The disembodied voices, dormant for a brief moment, now stirred with an uneasy murmuring that hinted at an ancient malevolence preparing to surge forth.

Isabella, attuned to the supernatural currents, sensed a disturbance that transcended the mundane. The cosmic energies that once whispered messages of guidance now crackled with an unsettling dissonance. The disembodied voices, their spectral murmurs now urgent and foreboding, conveyed that Ravenshade stood at the threshold of a perilous abyss.

Detective Harris, vigilant as ever, patrolled the town's streets, feeling the unsettling shift in the air. The mansion, once a bastion against malevolence, now seemed to harbor secrets that eluded his understanding. The disembodied voices, their whispers now a haunting melody carried by the night winds, insinuated that Detective Harris held the key to unveiling the ancient mysteries hidden within Ravenshade.

Victor, marked by the vampiric curse and the lingering energies of battles fought, felt the ominous tremors in his immortal core. The mansion, once a sanctuary, exuded a darkness that mirrored the haunting echoes of his past. The disembodied voices, recognizing Victor's unique connection to the supernatural, whispered fragments of a forgotten prophecy that foretold of an imminent reckoning.

As the trio delved into the mansion's enigmatic depths, they discovered forgotten chambers that echoed with the whispers of ancient spells. The artifact, once subdued, pulsed with a malevolent energy that sought to break free. The disembodied voices, now a disconcerting chorus reverberating through hidden passages, conveyed that the town's fate was intricately woven with the malevolence that lurked within.

In their quest for answers, Isabella, Victor, and Detective Harris stumbled upon an ancient grimoire detailing rituals that could either banish the malevolence or unleash its wrath. Symbols were etched, and incantations were uttered in an attempt to fortify Ravenshade against the impending darkness. The mansion resisted, its walls seemingly alive with unseen forces resisting the trio's efforts. The disembodied voices, their ethereal whispers now a symphony of despair, echoed through the hidden corridors, urging caution.

The rituals, while powerful, unveiled glimpses of the malevolent force attempting to breach the supernatural barriers. Shadows within the mansion writhed with an unnatural sentience, and the disembodied voices, their spectral chorus now a dirge, warned that Ravenshade's defenses were tested by an ancient adversary seeking retribution.

As the trio stood united against the looming threat, the mansion quaked with an otherworldly force. Shadows converged into a spectral entity that mirrored the very malevolence they sought to quell. The disembodied voices, their haunting melody now a desperate plea for salvation, guided the trio in a final stand against the encroaching darkness.

The mansion's grand halls became the stage for a surreal cosmic battle. Shadows clashed, and echoes of Ravenshade's history played out in ethereal flashes. The disembodied voices, their spectral chorus now a requiem, conveyed that the town's destiny rested on the trio's ability to thwart the impending malevolence.

Isabella, drawing upon her connection to the supernatural, reached into the very fabric of Ravenshade's essence. The spectral entity recoiled, its ethereal form quivering in the face of Isabella's newfound command over the cosmic forces. The disembodied voices, recognizing Isabella's pivotal role in the town's transformative journey, whispered words of empowerment and a promise of resilience.

Victor, marked by the vampiric curse and ancient energies, confronted the spectral entity with a renewed determination. His immortal existence, once a source of isolation, became a beacon of resistance against the encroaching darkness. The disembodied voices, recognizing Victor's journey of redemption, echoed a chorus of support and encouragement.

Detective Harris, a mortal navigating the cosmic unknown, faced the shadows with a determination that defied rational explanation. The spectral entity seemed to waver in the face of his unwavering resolve. The disembodied voices, now a supportive presence that echoed through the spectral winds, conveyed that Detective Harris held the key to fortifying Ravenshade's defenses.

As the trio channeled their collective energy, a radiant glow enveloped them. The spectral entity, unable to withstand the unified resistance, dissipated into the cosmic winds. The disembodied voices, their ethereal chorus now a resolute anthem, echoed through the mansion, heralding a moment of triumph over the encroaching malevolence.

Ravenshade, once again, emerged from the brink of darkness. The mansion's grand halls, though marked by the cosmic battles, now stood as a testament to the town's resilience. The disembodied voices, their whispers now a gentle breeze that carried through the mansion, conveyed a sense of gratitude and farewell.

Isabella, Victor, and Detective Harris, having faced the malevolence that sought to engulf Ravenshade, walked through the moonlit streets with a shared sense of accomplishment. The town, though battered by the cosmic storms, bore the scars of its battles with newfound strength. The mansion, standing stoically on the edge of town, seemed to exhale a sigh of relief.

The disembodied voices, their echoes now a distant memory, left Ravenshade with a final message of caution. The town, though momentarily spared, remained intertwined with the supernatural currents that flowed beneath its surface. Isabella, Victor, and Detective Harris, having played their parts in preserving Ravenshade's delicate equilibrium, found themselves on the precipice of a new chapter – a chapter that would test their resilience in the face of an ever-evolving cosmic tapestry.

Days turned into weeks, and Ravenshade, seemingly restored to tranquility, carried the echoes of its supernatural battles. The mansion's grand halls, once the stage for cosmic confrontations, now stood as a symbol of the town's endurance. The disembodied voices, though silent, left an indelible imprint on Ravenshade's history, a testament to the intertwined destinies of the supernatural and the mundane.

Yet, as the trio sought solace in the newfound peace, a subtle undercurrent hinted at the fragility of their triumph. Isabella, in her moments of quiet reflection, detected faint ripples in the cosmic energies. The tapestry on the wall, though still, seemed to hold a spectral resonance that whispered of untold secrets. The disembodied voices, though dormant, left an unsettling sense that Ravenshade's journey was far from over.

Detective Harris, resuming his role as the town's protector, delved into the unsolved mysteries that lingered in the shadows. The mansion, once a font of malevolence, now harbored unanswered questions. The disembodied voices, their whispers now a spectral echo, guided Detective Harris toward forgotten corners of Ravenshade where the threads of the supernatural wove a complex tapestry of enigmatic patterns.

Victor, still grappling with the remnants of his vampiric past, sensed a subtle shift in the mansion's energies. Shadows clung to him like ethereal tendrils, whispering forgotten tales of ancient struggles. The disembodied voices, though muted, hinted at a destiny that intertwined Victor's existence with Ravenshade's cosmic tapestry.

Isabella, attuned to the ebb and flow of supernatural forces, found herself drawn to the mansion's hidden chambers. The tapestry on the wall seemed to ripple with unseen currents, as if revealing glimpses of a forgotten history. The disembodied voices, their whispers now a delicate thread in the cosmic weave, guided Isabella toward revelations that promised both enlightenment and peril.

As the days unfolded, Ravenshade experienced a deceptive calm. The mansion's grandeur, once a source of awe, now carried an air of quiet trepidation. The disembodied voices, though subdued, resonated through the town, urging the trio to delve deeper into the mysteries that lay beneath the surface.

Detective Harris, driven by an unyielding determination, unearthed ancient manuscripts that spoke of a cosmic balance teetering on the edge. The mansion, a repository of forgotten knowledge, seemed to hold the key to understanding the intricate dance between the supernatural and the mundane. The disembodied voices, their spectral echoes now a guiding compass, directed Detective Harris toward a revelation that could alter Ravenshade's destiny.

Victor, haunted by the echoes of his vampiric existence, sought solace in the mansion's shadows. The tapestry on the wall, a canvas of enigmatic symbols, whispered cryptic messages that only Victor could decipher. The disembodied voices, recognizing Victor's pivotal role in the unfolding drama, murmured secrets that hinted at the town's fate resting in the hands of the immortal.

Isabella, delving into her own connection with the supernatural, communed with the unseen forces that permeated Ravenshade. The mansion's hidden corridors echoed with ethereal chants, and the tapestry on the wall seemed to come alive with vibrant energies. The disembodied voices, their whispers now a harmonious melody, guided Isabella toward a revelation that would blur the boundaries between her mortal existence and the cosmic forces at play.

As the trio gathered within the mansion's grand halls, a celestial alignment cast an eerie glow upon Ravenshade. Symbols etched on the walls pulsed with arcane energy, and the disembodied voices, their chorus now a celestial hymn, foretold of an impending convergence that would test the very fabric of reality.

Unbeknownst to the trio, a cosmic rift began to manifest within the mansion. Shadows morphed into spectral entities, and the tapestry on the wall seemed to unravel as if mirroring the unraveling of the town's delicate equilibrium. The disembodied voices, their celestial whispers now tinged with urgency, warned of a malevolent force seeking to exploit the burgeoning chaos.

Isabella, Victor, and Detective Harris found themselves entwined in a cosmic dance as the mansion's hidden chambers transformed into a realm where reality and the supernatural collided. The tapestry on the wall, now a portal to unseen dimensions, beckoned them toward a confrontation with the malevolence that sought to breach the cosmic barriers.

The disembodied voices, their ethereal chorus now a symphony of warning, guided the trio through the ever-shifting corridors of the mansion. Each step resonated with a palpable tension, and the air crackled with the energies of a looming cosmic upheaval. Ravenshade, on the brink of an existential crisis, awaited the outcome of the trio's journey into the heart of the supernatural maelstrom.

As the trio confronted the malevolence that lurked within the mansion's depths, an otherworldly tempest erupted. Shadows coalesced into a formidable adversary, and the tapestry on the wall became a canvas for the cosmic struggle. The disembodied voices, their celestial chorus now a battle hymn, urged Isabella, Victor, and Detective Harris to stand firm against the encroaching darkness.

In a crescendo of ethereal energies, the mansion's grand halls became a battlefield where the trio faced the malevolence head-on. Spells were cast, symbols illuminated with radiant energy, and the very fabric of reality seemed to waver. The disembodied voices, their celestial whispers now a cacophony of defiance, echoed through the cosmic storm as Ravenshade hung in the balance.

Isabella, drawing upon her newfound command over the supernatural, channeled energies that clashed with the malevolence. Victor, marked by the vampiric curse, unleashed powers that resonated with ancient forces. Detective Harris, the mortal among immortals, stood resolute against the cosmic tempest. The disembodied voices, their ethereal chorus now a symphony of cosmic forces, guided the trio in a final push to restore the delicate equilibrium Ravenshade so desperately clung to.

As the cosmic storm reached its zenith, a blinding light enveloped the mansion. The malevolence recoiled, shadows dissipated, and the tapestry on the wall seemed to mend itself. The disembodied voices, their celestial whispers now a gentle breeze, conveyed a sense of accomplishment that reverberated through the town.

Ravenshade, though scarred by the cosmic battles, emerged from the tempest with newfound resilience. The mansion's grand halls, witness to the ebb and flow of supernatural forces, stood as a testament to the town's enduring spirit. The disembodied voices, their whispers now a serene melody, echoed through Ravenshade, leaving behind a town forever changed by the cosmic odyssey that unfolded within its historic walls.

Chapter 17: Sacrifices

Deep within the mansion's chambers, an unsettling stillness settled over Ravenshade. Isabella, Victor, and Detective Harris could feel the palpable tension in the air, as if the very fabric of reality trembled with an ominous anticipation. The once-familiar halls of the mansion now carried an otherworldly weight, casting long shadows that seemed to harbor secrets darker than ever before.

As nightfall draped the town in an eerie silence, the mansion's grandeur transformed into a labyrinth of foreboding corridors. The tapestry on the wall, once a witness to the town's struggles, now seemed to writhe with spectral energies, weaving a tale of impending dread. The disembodied voices, quiet for a fleeting moment, now whispered cryptic warnings that echoed through the haunted halls.

Isabella, attuned to the supernatural currents, sensed an unsettling disturbance that sent shivers down her spine. The cosmic energies, once a guide, now fluctuated with an erratic rhythm. The disembodied voices, their spectral murmurs now urgent and disconcerting, conveyed that Ravenshade teetered on the precipice of a malevolence more ancient and insidious than anything they had faced before.

Detective Harris, ever vigilant, patrolled the town's desolate streets, feeling the weight of the impending darkness. The mansion, once a bastion against malevolence, now loomed as a nexus of unfathomable horrors. The disembodied voices, their whispers now a haunting melody carried by the chilling night breeze, insinuated that Detective Harris held the key to unlocking the town's deepest, darkest secrets.

Victor, marked by the vampiric curse and the lingering echoes of cosmic battles, felt the ominous ripples in his immortal essence. The mansion, a sanctuary turned malevolent, exuded a darkness that mirrored the haunting echoes of his tortured past. The disembodied voices, recognizing Victor's unique connection to the supernatural, whispered fragments of an ancient prophecy that foretold of an imminent reckoning.

As the trio ventured into the mansion's enigmatic depths, they discovered forgotten chambers that seemed to pulse with malevolent energies. The artifact, once seemingly subdued, now radiated with an unholy fervor that sought to consume them. The disembodied voices, now a disconcerting chorus reverberating through hidden passages, warned that the town's fate was intricately woven with the malevolence that lurked within.

In their quest for answers, Isabella, Victor, and Detective Harris uncovered an ancient grimoire that revealed rituals both forbidden and perilous. Symbols were etched, and incantations echoed through the mansion's halls in an attempt to fortify Ravenshade against the impending darkness. The mansion resisted, its walls seemingly alive with unseen forces that sought to thwart the trio's efforts. The disembodied voices, their ethereal whispers now a symphony of despair, echoed through the hidden corridors, urging caution.

The rituals, while potent, unveiled glimpses of the malevolent force attempting to breach the supernatural barriers. Shadows within the mansion writhed with an unnatural sentience, and the disembodied voices, their spectral chorus now a dirge, warned that Ravenshade's defenses were tested by an ancient adversary seeking retribution.

As the trio stood united against the looming threat, the mansion quaked with an otherworldly force. Shadows converged into a spectral entity that mirrored the very malevolence they sought to quell. The disembodied voices, their haunting melody now a desperate plea for salvation, guided the trio in a final stand against the encroaching darkness.

The mansion's grand halls became the battleground for a surreal cosmic clash. Shadows clashed, and echoes of Ravenshade's history played out in ethereal flashes. The disembodied voices, their spectral chorus now a requiem, conveyed that the town's destiny rested on the trio's ability to thwart the impending malevolence.

Isabella, drawing upon her newfound command over the supernatural, channeled energies that clashed with the malevolence. Victor, marked by the vampiric curse, unleashed powers that resonated with ancient forces. Detective Harris, the mortal among immortals, stood resolute against the cosmic tempest. The disembodied voices, their ethereal chorus now a symphony of cosmic forces, guided the trio in a final push to restore the delicate equilibrium Ravenshade so desperately clung to.

As the cosmic storm reached its zenith, a blinding light enveloped the mansion. The malevolence recoiled, shadows dissipated, and the tapestry on the wall seemed to mend itself. The disembodied voices, their celestial whispers now a gentle breeze, conveyed a sense of accomplishment that reverberated through the town.

Ravenshade, though scarred by the cosmic battles, emerged from the tempest with newfound resilience. The mansion's grand halls, witness to the ebb and flow of supernatural forces, stood as a testament to the town's enduring spirit. The disembodied voices, their whispers now a serene melody, echoed through Ravenshade, leaving behind a town forever changed by the cosmic odyssey that unfolded within its historic walls.

Yet, as the trio cautiously emerged from the mansion, the unsettling quietude that settled over Ravenshade hinted at the lingering malevolence that clung to the town's essence. The tapestry on the wall, though mended, seemed to shimmer with spectral energies, and the disembodied voices, now a distant echo, left an unsettling premonition that Ravenshade's struggle against the supernatural was far from over.

Detective Harris, grappling with the revelations within the mansion's depths, delved into forgotten archives seeking answers. The town, once thought to be free from the clutches of malevolence, now bore scars that begged for understanding. The disembodied voices, though distant, murmured cryptic clues that pointed toward the town's intricate connection to an ancient cosmic tapestry.

Victor, burdened by the weight of his immortal existence, found himself haunted by visions that transcended time. The mansion, now a sanctuary turned crucible, held fragments of a forgotten history that entwined with his own. The disembodied voices, their echoes now a lingering presence in Victor's solitude, whispered of a destiny that reached beyond the grasp of mere mortals.

Isabella, the conduit between the supernatural and the mundane, sensed the residual energies that clung to Ravenshade's streets. The town, though outwardly calm, pulsed with a heartbeat of otherworldly mysteries. The disembodied voices, their whispers now a subtle undertone in the cosmic symphony, guided Isabella toward a revelation that could either save or doom the town she had sworn to protect.

As days turned into nights, Ravenshade grappled with the aftermath of the cosmic turmoil. The mansion, once a symbol of both salvation and peril, stood as a silent sentinel overlooking the town's destiny. The disembodied voices, their ethereal presence now an enigmatic muse, urged the trio to unravel the threads of the town's enigma. Isabella, Victor, and Detective Harris, bound by the shared ordeal, convened to decipher the cryptic messages that lingered within the very fabric of Ravenshade's existence.

The trio, driven by an unyielding resolve, explored the mansion's hidden archives. Ancient tomes whispered forgotten truths, revealing the town's entanglement with cosmic forces beyond mortal comprehension. The tapestry on the wall, its threads now a visual symphony of intertwined destinies, seemed to convey a narrative that transcended time. The disembodied voices, though faint, resonated through the dimly lit chambers, guiding the trio toward revelations that danced on the edge of sanity.

Detective Harris, wrestling with the enigmatic clues, unraveled a forgotten chapter in Ravenshade's history. The mansion, it appeared, served as a nexus for otherworldly energies long before the trio's arrival. The disembodied voices, their echoes now a spectral guide, hinted at a cosmic dance that spanned epochs, where the town became a stage for forces that defied mortal understanding.

Victor, burdened by the weight of his vampiric past, discovered echoes of his own existence within the mansion's archives. The tapestry on the wall, a mural of immortal struggles, seemed to reflect Victor's journey of redemption. The disembodied voices, recognizing Victor's pivotal role in the town's cosmic drama, whispered fragments of a prophecy that intertwined his destiny with Ravenshade's.

Isabella, embracing her role as Ravenshade's guardian, delved into the ethereal currents that pulsed beneath the town's surface. The mansion, a conduit for supernatural energies, revealed a cosmic symphony that resonated with the very essence of reality. The disembodied voices, their whispers now a cosmic melody, guided Isabella toward a revelation that could potentially unravel the intricacies of the town's supernatural tapestry.

As the trio pieced together the fragments of Ravenshade's cosmic puzzle, a sense of urgency pervaded the town. Unseen forces stirred in the shadows, and spectral echoes hinted at an impending celestial alignment. The tapestry on the wall, now a living tableau of cosmic energies, seemed to ripple with anticipation. The disembodied voices, their ethereal whispers now charged with urgency, conveyed that Ravenshade stood at the threshold of a cosmic convergence that could reshape its very existence.

Isabella, Victor, and Detective Harris, united by a common purpose, faced the approaching celestial alignment with a mixture of trepidation and determination. The mansion, once a sanctuary turned repository of cosmic secrets, beckoned them to its grand halls for a final reckoning. The disembodied voices, their spectral echoes now a prelude to cosmic revelation, urged the trio to prepare for a confrontation that would determine the fate of Ravenshade.

As the celestial alignment cast an otherworldly glow over the mansion, symbols etched on the walls pulsed with radiant energy. The tapestry on the wall, now a conduit for cosmic forces, seemed to transcend its physical form. The disembodied voices, their ethereal chorus now a celestial hymn, guided Isabella, Victor, and Detective Harris toward the epicenter of the supernatural maelstrom.

Within the mansion's grand halls, the trio found themselves at the epicenter of a cosmic tempest. The tapestry on the wall, now a living canvas of celestial energies, flickered with visions that transcended time and space. The disembodied voices, their spectral chorus now a crescendo, heralded the convergence of cosmic forces that would decide Ravenshade's destiny.

Isabella, drawing upon the newfound depths of her supernatural abilities, stood at the forefront of the cosmic storm.

The tapestry's threads responded to her command, weaving a narrative that bridged the mortal and the supernatural. The disembodied voices, recognizing Isabella as the linchpin of the celestial alignment, murmured ancient incantations that resonated through the mansion's echoing halls.

Victor, embracing the vampiric powers that marked his existence, confronted the cosmic tempest with a stoic resolve. The tapestry on the wall, a reflection of his immortal struggles, seemed to acknowledge his journey toward redemption. The disembodied voices, their whispers now a supportive undertone in the cosmic symphony, guided Victor to wield his powers in harmony with the celestial energies.

Detective Harris, the mortal entrusted with safeguarding Ravenshade, faced the cosmic storm with unyielding determination. The mansion, a bastion of both supernatural secrets and earthly mysteries, resonated with the echoes of his unwavering resolve. The disembodied voices, recognizing Detective Harris's pivotal role in balancing the cosmic scales, whispered words of encouragement that reverberated through the grand halls.

As the celestial alignment reached its zenith, the mansion became a nexus of cosmic energies. The tapestry on the wall, now a conduit for otherworldly forces, seemed to transcend the boundaries of reality. The disembodied voices, their spectral chorus now a symphony of cosmic harmony, guided the trio in a final ritual that would either solidify Ravenshade's place in the cosmic tapestry or unravel its delicate equilibrium.

Isabella, Victor, and Detective Harris, their fates now intertwined with the very fabric of the universe, channeled their collective energies into the cosmic convergence. The mansion's grand halls resonated with a kaleidoscope of ethereal lights, and the disembodied voices, their celestial chorus reaching a zenith, echoed through the dimensions as the trio endeavored to maintain the delicate balance between the mundane and the supernatural.

The celestial energies surged, intertwining with the very essence of Ravenshade. The tapestry on the wall, a conduit for cosmic forces, shimmered with radiant hues that painted a tableau of the town's cosmic destiny. The disembodied voices, their spectral whispers now harmonizing in a cosmic melody, guided the trio through the final moments of the celestial alignment.

As the ritual reached its culmination, Ravenshade seemed suspended in a timeless cosmic dance. The mansion's grand halls became a transcendent space where mortal and immortal, mundane and supernatural, converged in a delicate equilibrium. The tapestry on the wall, now an ethereal masterpiece, told a story of resilience, redemption, and the town's enduring connection to the cosmic tapestry.

Isabella, Victor, and Detective Harris, their roles in the cosmic drama solidified, felt the energies of the convergence weave through their very beings. The tapestry on the wall, a living testament to their struggles, reflected the transformation of Ravenshade's destiny. The disembodied voices, their celestial whispers now a serene melody, conveyed a sense of fulfillment that resonated through the town.

The celestial glow began to subside, and Ravenshade returned to the embrace of its nocturnal normalcy. The mansion, once a focal point of supernatural mysteries, retained an air of quiet reverence. The tapestry on the wall, though no longer pulsating with cosmic energies, bore the imprints of the town's cosmic odyssey. The disembodied voices, now a gentle breeze that caressed Ravenshade, left behind a legacy of cosmic harmony.

In the aftermath of the celestial alignment, Ravenshade experienced a subtle transformation. The townsfolk, unaware of the cosmic struggles that unfolded within the mansion's walls, felt an intangible shift in the town's aura. The tapestry of everyday life seemed interwoven with newfound resilience, and the disembodied voices, their spectral echoes now a distant murmur, lingered as a reminder of the town's enduring connection to the supernatural.

Isabella, Victor, and Detective Harris, their destinies now entwined with Ravenshade's cosmic tapestry, found solace in the quiet moments that followed. The mansion, a silent witness to the town's struggles, stood as a sentinel of cosmic harmony. The tapestry on the wall, though no longer alive with celestial energies, conveyed a narrative of redemption and the triumph of the town's indomitable spirit.

As days turned into nights, Ravenshade embraced its newfound equilibrium. The mansion, once a source of both terror and sanctuary, became a symbol of the town's resilience in the face of cosmic challenges. The tapestry on the wall, though no longer animated by supernatural forces, retained its mystique, inviting the curious to contemplate the cosmic journey that unfolded within its intricate threads.

The disembodied voices, now a distant echo in the collective memory of Ravenshade, left an indelible mark on the town's consciousness. The celestial alignment, a chapter in the town's cosmic saga, became a part of Ravenshade's lore, whispered in hushed tones by those who sensed the lingering presence of the supernatural.

And so, Ravenshade stood at the crossroads of the mundane and the cosmic, forever marked by the tapestry on the wall that bore witness to the town's journey through the veil of the unknown. The mansion, with its hidden chambers and enigmatic symbols, became a testament to the enduring connection between mortals and the cosmic forces that shape their destinies. The disembodied voices, though now mere echoes in the town's memory, lingered as a reminder that, in the heart of Ravenshade, the line between reality and the supernatural was forever blurred.

Chapter 18: The Turning Point

In the aftermath of the celestial alignment, Ravenshade found itself shrouded in an uneasy tranquility. The once-familiar streets, now bathed in the soft glow of moonlight, concealed the residual echoes of cosmic energies that lingered like silent specters.

Isabella, Victor, and Detective Harris, though relieved by the apparent calm, sensed an undercurrent of disquiet. The mansion, once a focal point of supernatural tumult, stood in silent vigil over the town. The tapestry on the wall, stripped of its cosmic animation, seemed to harbor secrets that transcended the mortal realm. The disembodied voices, their whispers now a subtle breeze, hinted at the latent forces that still stirred beneath the surface.

As Ravenshade settled into an eerie quietude, reports of strange occurrences began to trickle in. Residents spoke of unsettling dreams that echoed the town's cosmic struggles. Shadows danced with an otherworldly sentience, and the air crackled with an unspoken tension. The tapestry on the wall, though seemingly dormant, retained an enigmatic quality that fueled the townsfolk's apprehensions. The disembodied voices, their echoes now a disconcerting murmur, suggested that the cosmic equilibrium forged in the mansion's depths might have unintended consequences.

Isabella, Victor, and Detective Harris, attuned to the town's pulse, embarked on a quest to uncover the source of the burgeoning unease. The mansion, its hidden chambers now cloaked in an ominous stillness, awaited their return. The tapestry on the wall, its threads seemingly restless, hinted at a disturbance that defied explanation. The disembodied voices, their spectral whispers now tinged with urgency, guided the trio toward the heart of Ravenshade's burgeoning dread.

In their exploration, the trio encountered manifestations of the supernatural that defied rational explanation. Shadows, once passive observers, now seemed imbued with a malevolent sentience that sought to ensnare the unwary. The mansion's corridors, once a sanctuary, became a labyrinth of disorienting twists and turns. The tapestry on the wall, though devoid of celestial animation, seemed to warp and ripple with unseen forces. The disembodied voices, their spectral murmurs now a haunting chorus, warned of an encroaching darkness that sought to unravel the fragile threads of the town's newfound equilibrium.

Residents of Ravenshade, gripped by an escalating sense of dread, began to recount encounters with apparitions that materialized in the moonlit hours. Whispers of forgotten prophecies echoed through the town, and the once-cozy atmosphere now carried an air of foreboding. The tapestry on the wall, its intricate patterns now seemingly rearranging themselves, mirrored the town's descent into supernatural turmoil. The disembodied voices, their ethereal whispers now a desperate plea, urged Isabella, Victor, and Detective Harris to confront the malevolence that threatened to plunge Ravenshade into an abyss of cosmic despair.

As the trio delved deeper into the mansion's enigmatic chambers, they uncovered forgotten rituals that hinted at a darker side of the celestial alignment. Symbols etched in ancient manuscripts pulsated with an unholy fervor, and incantations echoed through the mansion's dimly lit halls. The tapestry on the wall, its threads now weaving a tapestry of dread, seemed to absorb the malevolent energies that permeated the hidden spaces. The disembodied voices, their spectral whispers now a cacophony of warning, conveyed that the town's cosmic struggles were far from over.

Ravenshade, caught in the grip of supernatural turmoil, witnessed the emergence of otherworldly entities that defied description. The mansion, once a bastion against malevolence, now exuded an aura of spectral malevolence that seeped into the town's very foundations. The tapestry on the wall, now a canvas of cosmic nightmares, bore witness to the town's descent into the unknown. The disembodied voices, their ethereal chorus now a lament, guided the trio through a nightmarish odyssey that would test the limits of their resolve.

As the malevolence within Ravenshade reached a crescendo, the mansion's grand halls became a battleground where shadows coalesced into nightmarish entities. The tapestry on the wall, a reflection of the town's cosmic struggles, seemed to unravel as if mirroring the fraying sanity of its inhabitants. The disembodied voices, their spectral whispers now a mournful dirge, guided Isabella, Victor, and Detective Harris in a desperate struggle against the encroaching darkness.

Isabella, drawing upon her supernatural abilities, confronted the malevolent entities with a determination born of cosmic purpose. The tapestry on the wall, though tainted by the town's descent into darkness, responded to her command with flickering symbols that struggled to hold onto their celestial essence. The disembodied voices, their ethereal chorus now a plea for salvation, urged Isabella to channel the cosmic energies and quell the supernatural tempest that threatened to consume Ravenshade.

Victor, tormented by the echoes of his vampiric past, unleashed powers that resonated with ancient forces. The mansion's grand halls became a battleground where shadows clashed with the immortal's resolve. The tapestry on the wall, a testament to Victor's struggle for redemption, seemed to absorb the vampiric energies that surged through the cosmic maelstrom. The disembodied voices, recognizing Victor's pivotal role in the cosmic drama, murmured cryptic incantations that echoed through the supernatural battleground.

Detective Harris, the mortal thrust into the heart of the supernatural storm, stood resolute against the encroaching darkness. The mansion's hidden chambers, now a battleground between the mundane and the otherworldly, bore witness to the detective's unwavering determination. The tapestry on the wall, though marred by cosmic strife, seemed to ripple with the echoes of Detective Harris's mortal defiance. The disembodied voices, their spectral whispers now a rallying cry, guided the detective in a final stand against the malevolent forces that sought to claim Ravenshade's soul.

As the trio confronted the malevolent entities within the mansion, a cosmic tempest erupted. Shadows morphed into nightmarish apparitions, and the very fabric of reality seemed to unravel. The tapestry on the wall, though tainted by the town's descent into darkness, became a focal point of cosmic energies that pulsed with an otherworldly rhythm. The disembodied voices, their ethereal chorus now a symphony of despair, guided Isabella, Victor, and Detective Harris in a final push to restore the delicate equilibrium Ravenshade so desperately clung to.

In a climactic confrontation, the mansion's grand halls became a surreal battleground where the trio faced the malevolent entities head-on. Spells were cast, symbols illuminated with radiant energy, and the very fabric of reality seemed to waver. The tapestry on the wall, though tainted by cosmic strife, became a canvas for the town's desperate struggle against the encroaching darkness. The disembodied voices, their spectral whispers now a cacophony of defiance, echoed through the cosmic storm as Ravenshade hung in the balance.

Isabella, Victor, and Detective Harris found themselves entwined in a cosmic dance as the mansion's hidden chambers transformed into a realm where reality and the supernatural collided. The tapestry on the wall, now a portal to unseen dimensions, beckoned them toward a confrontation with the malevolence that sought to breach the cosmic barriers.

The battle within the mansion's grand halls intensified as the trio faced nightmarish apparitions fueled by malevolent energies. The tapestry on the wall, a focal point of cosmic struggle, seemed to pulsate with each clash, as if absorbing the very essence of the supernatural turmoil. The disembodied voices, their spectral chorus now a desperate plea for salvation, guided the trio through the shifting tides of the supernatural battleground.

Isabella, drawing upon the depths of her supernatural abilities, unleashed a surge of celestial energies that clashed with the malevolent entities. The tapestry on the wall, though tainted by the cosmic maelstrom, responded with flickering symbols that mirrored the ebb and flow of the supernatural battle. The disembodied voices, their ethereal whispers now a symphony of determination, urged Isabella to press forward and reclaim the town's cosmic equilibrium.

Victor, marked by the vampiric curse, confronted the nightmarish entities with a stoic resolve. Shadows recoiled in the face of his immortal powers, and the mansion's grand halls became a stage for a cosmic dance between the living and the undead. The tapestry on the wall, though frayed by the supernatural tempest, seemed to resonate with Victor's immortal struggle for redemption. The disembodied voices, recognizing Victor's pivotal role in the cosmic drama, whispered fragments of an ancient prophecy that hinted at the immortal's destiny.

Detective Harris, the mortal caught in the crossfire of the supernatural clash, stood resolute against the encroaching darkness. The mansion's hidden chambers, now a battleground for forces beyond mortal comprehension, bore witness to the detective's unwavering determination. The tapestry on the wall, though tainted by the cosmic strife, seemed to ripple with the echoes of Detective Harris's mortal defiance. The disembodied voices, their spectral whispers now a rallying cry, guided the detective in a final stand against the malevolent forces that sought to claim Ravenshade's soul.

As the trio pushed deeper into the mansion's enigmatic depths, the supernatural battleground intensified. Arcane energies crackled through the air, and the very walls seemed to vibrate with unseen forces. The tapestry on the wall, now a canvas for the town's cosmic struggles, became a conduit for the malevolent entities that sought to breach the town's fragile defenses. The disembodied voices, their ethereal chorus now a cacophony of warning, guided the trio toward a revelation that would either save Ravenshade or plunge it into eternal darkness.

In a climactic confrontation, Isabella, Victor, and Detective Harris faced the malevolent entities at the heart of the mansion. Spells were cast, symbols illuminated with radiant energy, and the very fabric of reality seemed to waver. The tapestry on the wall, though tainted by cosmic strife, became a focal point of cosmic energies that pulsed with an otherworldly rhythm. The disembodied voices, their ethereal chorus now a symphony of despair, echoed through the cosmic storm as Ravenshade hung in the balance.

Isabella, channeling the depths of her supernatural abilities, conjured a barrier of celestial energy that clashed with the malevolent entities. The tapestry on the wall, though marred by the supernatural tempest, responded with a celestial glow that mirrored the ebb and flow of the cosmic battle. The disembodied voices, their ethereal whispers now a desperate plea for salvation, guided Isabella in a final push to restore the town's cosmic equilibrium.

Victor, marked by the vampiric curse, confronted the nightmarish entities with a stoic resolve. Shadows recoiled in the face of his immortal powers, and the mansion's grand halls became a stage for a cosmic dance between the living and the undead. The tapestry on the wall, though frayed by the supernatural tempest, seemed to resonate with Victor's immortal struggle for redemption. The disembodied voices, recognizing Victor's pivotal role in the cosmic drama, whispered fragments of an ancient prophecy that hinted at the immortal's destiny.

Detective Harris, the mortal caught in the crossfire of the supernatural clash, stood resolute against the encroaching darkness. The mansion's hidden chambers, now a battleground for forces beyond mortal comprehension, bore witness to the detective's unwavering determination. The tapestry on the wall, though tainted by the cosmic strife, seemed to ripple with the echoes of Detective Harris's mortal defiance. The disembodied voices, their spectral whispers now a rallying cry, guided the detective in a final stand against the malevolent forces that sought to claim Ravenshade's soul.

As the trio pushed deeper into the mansion's enigmatic depths, the supernatural battleground intensified. Arcane energies crackled through the air, and the very walls seemed to vibrate with unseen forces. The tapestry on the wall, now a canvas for the town's cosmic struggles, became a conduit for the malevolent entities that sought to breach the town's fragile defenses. The disembodied voices, their ethereal chorus now a cacophony of warning, guided the trio toward a revelation that would either save Ravenshade or plunge it into eternal darkness.

In a climactic confrontation, Isabella, Victor, and Detective Harris faced the malevolent entities at the heart of the mansion. Spells were cast, symbols illuminated with radiant energy, and the very fabric of reality seemed to waver. The tapestry on the wall, though tainted by cosmic strife, became a focal point of cosmic energies that pulsed with an otherworldly rhythm. The disembodied voices, their ethereal chorus now a symphony of despair, echoed through the cosmic storm as Ravenshade hung in the balance.

Isabella, channeling the depths of her supernatural abilities, conjured a barrier of celestial energy that clashed with the malevolent entities. The tapestry on the wall, though marred by the supernatural tempest, responded with a celestial glow that mirrored the ebb and flow of the cosmic battle. The disembodied voices, their ethereal whispers now a desperate plea for salvation, guided Isabella in a final push to restore the town's cosmic equilibrium.

Victor, marked by the vampiric curse, confronted the nightmarish entities with a stoic resolve. Shadows recoiled in the face of his immortal powers

Chapter 19: The Confrontation

The supernatural tempest within the mansion reached a fever pitch as Isabella, Victor, and Detective Harris confronted the malevolent entities at the heart of Ravenshade's cosmic struggles. Arcane energies crackled in the air, casting eerie shadows on the walls. The tapestry on the wall, once a reflection of the town's cosmic drama, seemed to writhe with a sinister life of its own.

Isabella, fueled by a determination born of cosmic purpose, stood at the forefront, channeling celestial energies to create a protective barrier. The malevolent entities, their forms a twisted manifestation of darkness, clashed against the celestial defenses. The mansion's grand halls became a battleground where supernatural forces clashed with an intensity that sent shivers down the spines of the trio.

Victor, embracing the vampiric powers that marked his existence, confronted the nightmarish entities with stoic resolve. Shadows recoiled in the face of his immortal powers, and the very air became charged with an otherworldly tension. The tapestry on the wall, though tainted by the cosmic tempest, seemed to resonate with Victor's immortal struggle for redemption. The disembodied voices, recognizing Victor's pivotal role in the cosmic drama, whispered fragments of an ancient prophecy that hinted at the immortal's destiny.

Detective Harris, the mortal thrust into the heart of the supernatural storm, stood resolute against the encroaching darkness. The mansion's hidden chambers, now a battleground for forces beyond mortal comprehension, bore witness to the detective's unwavering determination. The tapestry on the wall, though marred by the cosmic strife, seemed to ripple with the echoes of Detective Harris's mortal defiance. The disembodied voices, their spectral whispers now a rallying cry, guided the detective in a final stand against the malevolent forces that sought to claim Ravenshade's soul.

As the trio pushed deeper into the mansion's enigmatic depths, the supernatural battleground intensified. Arcane energies crackled through the air, and the very walls seemed to vibrate with unseen forces. The tapestry on the wall, now a canvas for the town's cosmic struggles, became a conduit for the malevolent entities that sought to breach the town's fragile defenses. The disembodied voices, their ethereal chorus now a cacophony of warning, guided the trio toward a revelation that would either save Ravenshade or plunge it into eternal darkness.

In a climactic confrontation, Isabella, Victor, and Detective Harris faced the malevolent entities at the heart of the mansion. Spells were cast, symbols illuminated with radiant energy, and the very fabric of reality seemed to waver. The tapestry on the wall, though tainted by cosmic strife, became a focal point of cosmic energies that pulsed with an otherworldly rhythm. The disembodied voices, their ethereal chorus now a symphony of despair, echoed through the cosmic storm as Ravenshade hung in the balance.

Isabella, channeling the depths of her supernatural abilities, conjured a barrier of celestial energy that clashed with the 2malevolent entities. The tapestry on the wall, though marred by the supernatural tempest, responded with a celestial glow that mirrored the ebb and flow of the cosmic battle. The disembodied voices, their ethereal whispers now a desperate plea for salvation, guided Isabella in a final push to restore the town's cosmic equilibrium.

Victor, marked by the vampiric curse, confronted the nightmarish entities with a stoic resolve. Shadows recoiled in the face of his immortal powers, and the mansion's grand halls became a stage for a cosmic dance between the living and the undead. The tapestry on the wall, though frayed by the supernatural tempest, seemed to resonate with Victor's immortal struggle for redemption. The disembodied voices, recognizing Victor's pivotal role in the cosmic drama, whispered fragments of an ancient prophecy that hinted at the immortal's destiny.

Detective Harris, the mortal caught in the crossfire of the supernatural clash, stood resolute against the encroaching darkness. The mansion's hidden chambers, now a battleground for forces beyond mortal comprehension, bore witness to the detective's unwavering determination. The tapestry on the wall, though tainted by the cosmic strife, seemed to ripple with the echoes of Detective Harris's mortal defiance. The disembodied voices, their spectral whispers now a rallying cry, guided the detective in a final stand against the malevolent forces that sought to claim Ravenshade's soul.

As the trio pushed deeper into the mansion's enigmatic depths, the supernatural battleground intensified. Arcane energies crackled through the air, and the very walls seemed to vibrate with unseen forces. The tapestry on the wall, now a canvas for the town's cosmic struggles, became a conduit for the malevolent entities that sought to breach the town's fragile defenses. The disembodied voices, their ethereal chorus now a cacophony of warning, guided the trio toward a revelation that would either save Ravenshade or plunge it into eternal darkness.

In a climactic confrontation, Isabella, Victor, and Detective Harris faced the malevolent entities at the heart of the mansion. Spells were cast, symbols illuminated with radiant energy, and the very fabric of reality seemed to waver. The tapestry on the wall, though tainted by cosmic strife, became a focal point of cosmic energies that pulsed with an otherworldly rhythm. The disembodied voices, their ethereal chorus now a symphony of despair, echoed through the cosmic storm as Ravenshade hung in the balance.

Isabella, channeling the depths of her supernatural abilities, conjured a barrier of celestial energy that clashed with the malevolent entities. The tapestry on the wall, though marred by the supernatural tempest, responded with a celestial glow that mirrored the ebb and flow of the cosmic battle. The disembodied voices, their ethereal whispers now a desperate plea for salvation, guided Isabella in a final push to restore the town's cosmic equilibrium.

Victor, marked by the vampiric curse, confronted the nightmarish entities with a stoic resolve. Shadows recoiled in the face of his immortal powers, and the mansion's grand halls became a stage for a cosmic dance between the living and the undead. The tapestry on the wall, though frayed by the supernatural tempest, seemed to resonate with Victor's immortal struggle for redemption. The disembodied voices, recognizing Victor's pivotal role in the cosmic drama, whispered fragments of an ancient prophecy that hinted at the immortal's destiny.

Detective Harris, the mortal caught in the crossfire of the supernatural clash, stood resolute against the encroaching darkness. The mansion's hidden chambers, now a battleground for forces beyond mortal comprehension, bore witness to the detective's unwavering determination. The tapestry on the wall, though tainted by the cosmic strife, seemed to ripple with the echoes of danger/

Detective Harris's mortal defiance. The disembodied voices, their spectral whispers now a rallying cry, guided the detective in a final stand against the malevolent forces that sought to claim Ravenshade's soul.

As the trio pressed forward, the very fabric of reality seemed to unravel within the mansion's mysterious depths. The air crackled with arcane energies, casting eerie shadows that danced with malevolent intent. The tapestry on the wall, now a twisted tableau of cosmic horrors, pulsed with an unsettling rhythm that mirrored the chaotic dance of the supernatural forces at play.

Isabella, Victor, and Detective Harris found themselves entangled in a surreal nightmare as the malevolent entities intensified their assault. The mansion's grand halls, once a sanctuary, became a labyrinth of torment where each step echoed with the whispering echoes of unseen horrors. The tapestry on the wall, its threads now weaving a tapestry of dread, seemed to capture the essence of the trio's struggle against an ancient darkness.

Isabella, her celestial energies strained, felt the weight of the cosmic battle pressing down on her. The protective barrier wavered as the malevolent entities surged forward with renewed vigor. The tapestry on the wall, though marred by the supernatural tempest, emitted flickering symbols that mirrored the ebb and flow of the cosmic struggle. The disembodied voices, their ethereal whispers now a desperate plea for salvation, urged Isabella to find the strength within to overcome the encroaching darkness.

Victor, battling the shadows of his vampiric past, unleashed powers that resonated with ancient forces. The mansion's grand halls became a battleground where shadows coalesced into nightmarish entities. The tapestry on the wall, a testament to Victor's struggle for redemption, absorbed the vampiric energies that surged through the cosmic maelstrom. The disembodied voices, recognizing Victor's pivotal role in the cosmic drama, murmured cryptic incantations that echoed through the supernatural battleground.

Detective Harris, standing firm against the tide of malevolence, faced spectral entities that seemed to materialize from the very shadows. The mansion's hidden chambers, now a theater of the macabre, bore witness to the detective's mortal defiance. The tapestry on the wall, though marred by cosmic strife, seemed to ripple with the echoes of Detective Harris's unwavering determination. The disembodied voices, their spectral whispers now a haunting chorus, guided the detective in a final stand against the encroaching darkness.

As the trio battled through the mansion's surreal dimensions, the malevolent entities manifested in increasingly grotesque forms. Shapes twisted and contorted, and the very walls seemed to close in on them. The tapestry on the wall, now a shifting canvas of cosmic nightmares, bore witness to the town's descent into the unknown. The disembodied voices, their ethereal chorus now a lament, guided Isabella, Victor, and Detective Harris through a nightmarish odyssey that would test the limits of their resolve.

In the heart of the mansion's enigmatic depths, the trio encountered an ancient altar pulsating with dark energies. Symbols etched in forgotten tongues seemed to writhe with a malevolent sentience. The tapestry on the wall, its threads now weaving a tapestry of dread, seemed to resonate with the ominous presence that loomed over the cosmic battleground. The disembodied voices, their spectral murmurs now tinged with urgency, warned of an impending ritual that could tip the balance between the mortal and the supernatural.

As the trio deciphered the cryptic symbols and incantations, a revelation unfolded—a dark prophecy foretelling the convergence of cosmic forces that would either usher in a new era of malevolence or seal the town's fate in eternal darkness. The mansion, a conduit for ancient rituals, seemed to echo with the whispers of the past, each chamber revealing fragments of the town's haunted history.

Isabella, Victor, and Detective Harris, burdened by the weight of their destinies, realized that the only way to break the malevolent cycle was to confront the source of the ancient darkness—an otherworldly entity that thrived on the town's cosmic struggles. The tapestry on the wall, now a portal to unseen dimensions, beckoned them toward a confrontation with the malevolence that sought to breach the cosmic barriers.

The ritual's climax drew near as the trio delved deeper into the mansion's ominous core. Shadows morphed into nightmarish apparitions, and the very fabric of reality seemed to unravel. The tapestry on the wall, though tainted by cosmic strife, became a focal point of cosmic energies that pulsed with an otherworldly rhythm. The disembodied voices, their ethereal chorus now a symphony of despair, echoed through the cosmic storm as Ravenshade hung in the balance.

Isabella, Victor, and Detective Harris found themselves entwined in a cosmic dance as the mansion's hidden chambers transformed into a realm where reality and the supernatural collided. The tapestry on the wall, now a portal to unseen dimensions, beckoned them toward a confrontation with the malevolence that sought to breach the cosmic barriers.

The otherworldly entity, a manifestation of ancient darkness, materialized before the trio. Its form twisted and contorted, a grotesque amalgamation

of shadowy tendrils and ethereal whispers. The very air vibrated with its malevolent presence as it taunted the trio with cryptic riddles that echoed through the haunted halls.

Isabella, drawing upon the celestial energies within her, initiated a counter-ritual to disrupt the entity's dark convergence. The tapestry on the wall, though tainted by the malevolence that pulsed through the mansion, responded with flickering symbols that mirrored the ebb and flow of the cosmic struggle. The disembodied voices, their ethereal whispers now a symphony of determination, guided Isabella in a final push to thwart the impending doom.

Victor, embracing the vampiric powers that marked his existence, confronted the entity with a stoic resolve. Shadows recoiled in the face of his immortal powers, and the mansion's grand halls became a stage for a cosmic dance between the living and the undead. The tapestry on the wall, though frayed by the supernatural tempest, seemed to resonate with Victor's immortal struggle for redemption. The disembodied voices, recognizing Victor's pivotal role in the cosmic drama, whispered fragments of an ancient prophecy that hinted at the immortal's destiny.

Detective Harris, fueled by mortal determination, faced the entity with unwavering courage. The mansion's hidden chambers, now a battleground for forces beyond mortal comprehension, bore witness to the detective's mortal defiance. The tapestry on the wall, though marred by cosmic strife, seemed to ripple with the echoes of Detective Harris's resilience. The disembodied voices, their spectral whispers now a rallying cry, guided the detective in a final stand against the malevolent forces that sought to claim Ravenshade's soul.

The entity, enraged by the trio's defiance, unleashed a torrent of dark energies. The mansion shook as the cosmic storm intensified, threatening to engulf Ravenshade in eternal darkness. The tapestry on the wall, now a canvas for the town's cosmic struggles, seemed to warp and ripple with the onslaught of malevolence. The disembodied voices, their ethereal chorus now a desperate plea for salvation, urged the trio to endure the final onslaught.

As Isabella, Victor, and Detective Harris stood united against the entity, a surge of celestial and vampiric energies intertwined with mortal determination. The mansion's grand halls became a battlefield where cosmic forces clashed with an intensity that transcended mortal comprehension. The tapestry on the wall, though battered and torn, emitted a defiant glow that mirrored the trio's resilience. The disembodied voices, their spectral whispers now a symphony of hope, guided the trio through the final moments of the cosmic confrontation.

In a climactic surge of power, Isabella, Victor, and Detective Harris channeled their combined strengths to disrupt the entity's dark convergence. The mansion quivered as the malevolence recoiled, its shadowy tendrils dissipating into the cosmic void. The tapestry on the wall, though scarred by the supernatural tempest, emitted a radiant glow that resonated with the triumph of the trio over the ancient darkness. The disembodied voices, their ethereal chorus now a hymn of victory, echoed through the once-haunted halls.

Ravenshade, released from the grip of cosmic turmoil, gradually returned to a state of uneasy calm. The mansion, once a bastion of malevolence, stood silent as the cosmic storm subsided. The tapestry on the wall, now a testament to the town's resilience, hung as a reminder of the harrowing journey that had unfolded within its hidden chambers. The disembodied voices, their spectral whispers now fading into echoes, conveyed a sense of closure as the trio emerged from the cosmic ordeal.

Isabella, Victor, and Detective Harris, though physically and emotionally drained, felt a profound sense of accomplishment. The town, spared from an eternity of darkness, began to heal from the scars of the supernatural tempest. The tapestry on the wall, though forever marked by the cosmic struggles, became a symbol of Ravenshade's resilience in the face of ancient malevolence. The disembodied voices, their spectral whispers now a gentle breeze, carried with them a sense of gratitude as the trio gazed upon the town they had saved from the brink of cosmic despair.

As Ravenshade settled into a new chapter of its existence, Isabella, Victor, and Detective Harris knew that the echoes of their cosmic journey would linger in the town's collective memory. The mansion, now devoid of malevolence, stood as a testament to the trio's bravery in the face of ancient darkness. The tapestry on the wall, though forever marked by the cosmic struggles, became a living chronicle of Ravenshade's resilience in the face of supernatural turmoil. The disembodied voices, their spectral whispers now a fading echo, conveyed a sense of gratitude as the trio bid farewell to the once-haunted mansion, their cosmic odyssey etched into the very fabric of the town's history.

Chapter 20: Redemption

The aftermath of the cosmic confrontation left Ravenshade in an eerie calm. The once-haunted mansion, now devoid of malevolence, stood like a sentinel in the moonlit night. Isabella, Victor, and Detective Harris emerged from the grand halls, their faces etched with weariness but also a profound sense of accomplishment.

As the trio stepped into the cool night air, the town seemed to hold its breath. The tapestry on the wall, bearing the scars of the supernatural tempest, hung ominously. Its threads whispered tales of the cosmic struggles that had unfolded within the mansion's hidden chambers. The disembodied voices, now a faint echo, lingered as a reminder of the ordeal that had tested Ravenshade's very existence.

Yet, as the trio surveyed the tranquil town, a subtle unease lingered in the shadows. The supernatural storm had left an indelible mark on Ravenshade, and the echoes of ancient darkness seemed to reverberate through the silent streets. The tapestry on the wall, though radiant with the town's triumph, hinted at secrets that lay beneath its seemingly serene surface.

Isabella, sensing the residual energies that clung to Ravenshade, furrowed her brow. The celestial powers within her whispered of an unsettled equilibrium, and the mansion's grand halls still held traces of otherworldly vibrations. The tapestry on the wall, a silent witness to the cosmic struggle, seemed to shift in the moonlight, casting eerie shadows that danced with unseen forces.

The disembodied voices, their spectral whispers now tinged with uncertainty, guided the trio toward an unsettling realization.

Victor, ever attuned to the vampiric energies that flowed through his immortal veins, sensed a lingering darkness that clung to Ravenshade's very essence. The mansion's hidden chambers, though free from overt malevolence, echoed with traces of ancient malevolence. The tapestry on the wall, its threads now woven with the echoes of cosmic battles, seemed to ripple as if concealing a cosmic secret. The disembodied voices, their ethereal murmurs now a foreboding murmur, urged Victor to remain vigilant against the subtle undercurrents of supernatural unrest.

Detective Harris, still grappling with the memories of the harrowing ordeal, couldn't shake the feeling that Ravenshade's newfound calm was a fragile illusion. The mansion's grand halls, once a theater of cosmic struggles, bore witness to the detective's lingering unease. The tapestry on the wall, though a symbol of victory, hinted at the thin veil that separated the town from the unknown. The disembodied voices, their spectral whispers now a cautionary refrain, reminded Detective Harris that the cosmic odyssey might have merely scratched the surface of Ravenshade's mysteries.

As the trio ventured deeper into the heart of the town, the subtle disquiet intensified. Shadows flickered in the periphery, and the air felt charged with latent energies. The tapestry on the wall, though bathed in moonlight, seemed to absorb the shadows and warp into unsettling shapes. The disembodied voices, their ethereal chorus now a discordant melody, guided the trio toward the epicenter of the town's lingering cosmic unrest.

Isabella, Victor, and Detective Harris found themselves drawn to the town square, a place that had witnessed the culmination of the cosmic confrontation. The very ground beneath their feet seemed to pulse with residual energies. The tapestry on the wall, now a beacon of enigmatic illumination, cast eerie shadows on the cobblestone streets. The disembodied voices, their spectral whispers now urgent, guided the trio toward a revelation that promised to unveil the town's deepest secrets.

In the town square, a cryptic symbol manifested, etched in invisible energies that seemed to dance with ancient intent. The tapestry on the wall, its threads now quivering with unseen forces, mirrored the cryptic symbol as if unlocking a gateway to the unknown. The disembodied voices, their ethereal murmurs now a cryptic incantation, guided Isabella, Victor, and Detective Harris into a cosmic dance that would unravel Ravenshade's most guarded mysteries.

As the trio approached the cryptic symbol, the very air became charged with anticipation. Shadows converged, and the tapestry on the wall, now a living canvas of cosmic revelations, emitted a spectral glow that bathed the town square in an otherworldly light. The disembodied voices, their ethereal chorus now a crescendo of revelation, whispered secrets that echoed through the silent streets.

Isabella, channeling the depths of her celestial powers, traced the unseen lines of the cryptic symbol. The mansion's hidden chambers, though distant, seemed to respond with a subtle tremor. The tapestry on the wall, its threads now a conduit for cosmic energies, vibrated in resonance with Isabella's celestial invocation. The disembodied voices, their spectral whispers now a guiding hymn, unveiled fragments of an ancient prophecy that foretold Ravenshade's destiny.

Victor, attuned to the vampiric energies that lingered in the town square, felt a surge of immortal intuition. The cryptic symbol, though invisible to mortal eyes, pulsed with vampiric resonance. The tapestry on the wall, now a gateway to unseen realms, seemed to absorb the immortal energies that emanated from Victor's very being. The disembodied voices, their ethereal murmurs now a cryptic dialogue, hinted at the role Victor played in the cosmic tapestry that enveloped Ravenshade.

Detective Harris, ever the pragmatic observer, scrutinized the cryptic symbol with a detective's scrutiny. The town square, though seemingly tranquil, held clues that eluded mortal comprehension. The tapestry on the wall, now a mosaic of cosmic secrets, whispered fragments of an unsolved mystery that begged for Detective Harris's investigative prowess. The disembodied voices, their spectral whispers now a cryptic revelation, guided the detective toward the heart of Ravenshade's enigma.

As Isabella, Victor, and Detective Harris delved into the cosmic dance within the town square, the very fabric of reality seemed to warp. The cryptic symbol, now a focal point of unseen forces, shimmered with the convergence of celestial, vampiric and mortal energies. The tapestry on the wall, its threads now intricately woven with cosmic vibrations, pulsed with an otherworldly rhythm that echoed through the silent streets. The disembodied voices, their ethereal chorus now a harmonious blend of revelation, guided the trio toward a revelation that would redefine Ravenshade's understanding of its own existence.

In the midst of the cosmic dance, the cryptic symbol began to unveil hidden layers of meaning. Isabella, Victor, and Detective Harris found themselves entangled in a kaleidoscope of visions—a tapestry of Ravenshade's past, present, and future. The mansion's grand halls, though distant, manifested in spectral reflections that mirrored the trio's cosmic journey. The tapestry on the wall, now a living chronicle of the town's cosmic struggles, shifted with each revelation, bearing witness to the town's timeless narrative. The disembodied voices, their spectral whispers now an omniscient narrative, guided the trio through the cosmic tapestry that wove the fabric of Ravenshade's existence.

Isabella, glimpsing fragments of celestial insights, saw the interconnected threads of destiny that bound Ravenshade to cosmic forces. The cryptic symbol, etched in the town square, seemed to resonate with the celestial energies that flowed through Isabella's very essence. The tapestry on the wall, now a celestial canvas painted with ethereal hues, reflected the town's symbiotic relationship with the celestial realm. The disembodied voices, their ethereal whispers now a cosmic dialogue, conveyed a revelation that Ravenshade's fate was intricately intertwined with celestial machinations.

Victor, tapping into the vampiric intuition that marked his immortal existence, perceived the cryptic symbol as a vampiric sigil—an ancient mark that signified the town's connection to the realm of the undead. The tapestry on the wall, now a canvas painted with vampiric shadows, hinted at the role Victor played in shaping Ravenshade's immortal destiny. The disembodied voices, their ethereal murmurs now a vampiric chant, unveiled the revelation that the town's fate had been guided by immortal forces beyond mortal comprehension.

Detective Harris, interpreting the cryptic symbol through the lens of earthly scrutiny, discerned patterns that hinted at Ravenshade's mortal history. The town square, though infused with cosmic energies, held echoes of mortal struggles that shaped Ravenshade's identity. The tapestry on the wall, now a mosaic of mortal tales, conveyed the resilience of Ravenshade's inhabitants in the face of supernatural adversity. The disembodied voices, their spectral whispers now a mortal narrative, revealed that the town's survival depended on the resilience of its mortal inhabitants.

As the revelations unfolded, the cryptic symbol pulsed with an intensity that transcended the boundaries of time and space. The tapestry on the wall, now a living chronicle of Ravenshade's cosmic journey, seemed to stretch beyond the confines of the town square, reaching into unseen dimensions. The disembodied voices, their ethereal chorus now a universal melody, guided the trio toward a revelation that transcended the distinctions between celestial, vampiric, and mortal.

Isabella, Victor, and Detective Harris, their senses attuned to the cosmic revelations, felt a profound connection to Ravenshade's timeless narrative. The cryptic symbol, now a beacon of cosmic resonance, served as a bridge between the town's past, present, and future. The tapestry on the wall, though scarred by cosmic struggles, shimmered with a radiant glow that symbolized the unity of celestial, vampiric, and mortal forces. The disembodied voices, their ethereal whispers now a cosmic anthem, conveyed the revelation that Ravenshade's destiny was a cosmic symphony conducted by unseen hands.

In the climax of the cosmic dance, the cryptic symbol reached a crescendo of energy, unleashing a surge that reverberated through Ravenshade. The tapestry on the wall, now an ethereal tableau of cosmic harmony, emitted a radiant glow that bathed the town square in celestial light. The disembodied voices, their spectral chorus now a triumphant hymn, heralded the revelation that Ravenshade had transcended its haunted past to become a nexus of cosmic balance.

As Isabella, Victor, and Detective Harris absorbed the cosmic revelations, a profound sense of purpose settled upon them. The cryptic symbol, now an integral part of Ravenshade's cosmic tapestry, faded into the fabric of the town square. The tapestry on the wall, though forever marked by cosmic struggles, exuded a sense of cosmic equilibrium that transcended the boundaries of the supernatural.

In the aftermath of the cosmic revelation, Ravenshade embraced a new era—a synthesis of celestial, vampiric, and mortal influences. The mansion, once a bastion of malevolence, stood as a testament to the town's resilience in the face of cosmic adversity. The tapestry on the wall, though scarred by supernatural tempests, hung as a cosmic mural that celebrated Ravenshade's journey through the ages. The disembodied voices, their spectral whispers now a cosmic lullaby, conveyed a sense of peace as the town basked in the newfound harmony of its cosmic existence.

The cryptic symbol in the town square pulsed with an eerie energy, casting shadows that danced like malevolent spirits. Isabella, Victor, and Detective Harris, despite their weariness, felt an unspoken tension in the air. The tapestry on the wall, marked by the recent cosmic revelations, hung ominously, its threads seemingly alive with unseen forces. The disembodied voices, once a guiding presence, now murmured in an unsettling cadence, as if warning of the impending revelation that lingered within the cryptic symbol.

As the trio approached the symbol, each step seemed to echo through the town square like a distant drumbeat. Isabella, with her celestial insight, sensed an otherworldly resonance emanating from the cryptic symbol. The tapestry on the wall, though radiant with recent revelations, cast shadows that seemed to writhe with celestial unease. The disembodied voices, their ethereal whispers now tinged with uncertainty, guided Isabella toward the cryptic heart of Ravenshade's cosmic mysteries.

Victor, attuned to the vampiric energies that lingered in the town square, felt a chill down his immortal spine. The cryptic symbol, though invisible to most, pulsed with an undeniable vampiric presence. The tapestry on the wall, a canvas painted with the town's cosmic struggles, seemed to absorb the shadows that clung to Victor's immortal existence. The disembodied voices, their spectral murmurs now a foreboding chant, urged Victor to be vigilant against the unseen forces that lurked within the cryptic symbol.

Detective Harris, guided by earthly intuition, scrutinized the symbol with a detective's skepticism. The town square, despite its apparent tranquility, held an undercurrent of mysterious energies. The tapestry on the wall, now a mosaic of cosmic secrets, whispered fragments of an unsolved mystery that beckoned Detective Harris's investigative instincts. The disembodied voices, their spectral whispers now a cryptic revelation, guided the detective toward the heart of Ravenshade's enigma.

As the trio reached the center of the town square, the cryptic symbol seemed to intensify in its enigmatic glow. Shadows gathered, and the air grew thick with anticipation. The tapestry on the wall, though a testament to recent cosmic revelations, now warped with unsettling shapes that seemed to mirror the cosmic unease. The disembodied voices, their ethereal chorus now a dissonant melody, guided the trio toward the cryptic climax that awaited them.

Isabella, reaching out with celestial energies, traced the unseen lines of the cryptic symbol. The mansion's hidden chambers, though distant, responded with a subtle tremor. The tapestry on the wall, its threads now a conduit for cosmic energies, vibrated in resonance with Isabella's celestial invocation. The disembodied voices, their spectral whispers now a guiding hymn, unveiled fragments of an ancient prophecy that hinted at Ravenshade's destiny.

Victor, feeling the vampiric pulse of the symbol, sensed an impending revelation. The cryptic symbol, though invisible to mortal eyes, pulsed with vampiric resonance that sent shivers through his immortal form. The tapestry on the wall, now a gateway to unseen realms, seemed to absorb the immortal energies that emanated from Victor's very being. The disembodied voices, their ethereal murmurs now a vampiric chant, hinted at the role Victor played in the cosmic tapestry that enveloped Ravenshade.

Detective Harris, eyeing the symbol with a detective's scrutiny, discerned patterns that hinted at Ravenshade's mortal history. The town square, though seemingly tranquil, held clues that eluded mortal comprehension. The tapestry on the wall, now a mosaic of mortal tales, conveyed the resilience of Ravenshade's inhabitants in the face of supernatural adversity. The disembodied voices, their spectral whispers now a mortal narrative, revealed that the town's survival depended on the resilience of its mortal inhabitants.

As the revelations unfolded, the cryptic symbol pulsed with an intensity that transcended the boundaries of time and space. The tapestry on the wall, now an intricately woven canvas of Ravenshade's cosmic journey, seemed to stretch beyond the confines of the town square, reaching into unseen dimensions. The disembodied voices, their ethereal chorus now a universal melody, guided the trio toward a revelation that transcended the distinctions between celestial, vampiric, and mortal.

Isabella, Victor, and Detective Harris, their senses attuned to the cosmic revelations, felt a profound connection to Ravenshade's timeless narrative. The cryptic symbol, now an integral part of Ravenshade's cosmic tapestry, faded into the fabric of the town square. The tapestry on the wall, though forever marked by cosmic struggles, exuded a sense of cosmic equilibrium that transcended the boundaries of the supernatural.

In the aftermath of the cosmic revelation, Ravenshade embraced a new era—a synthesis of celestial, vampiric, and mortal influences. The mansion, once a bastion of malevolence, stood as a testament to the town's resilience in the face of cosmic adversity. The tapestry on the wall, though scarred by supernatural tempests, hung as a cosmic mural that celebrated Ravenshade's journey through the ages. The disembodied voices, their spectral whispers now a cosmic lullaby, conveyed a sense of peace as the town basked in the newfound harmony of its cosmic existence.

www.ingramcontent.com/pod-product-compliance
Lightning Source LLC
Chambersburg PA
CBHW071417150726
48000CB00001B/373